crystals
talk to the
woman within

crystals

talk to the
woman within

teach yourself to rely on her support

cassandra eason

quantum

LONDON • NEW YORK • TORONTO • SYDNEY

quantum

An imprint of W. Foulsham & Co. Ltd
The Publishing House, Bennetts Close,
Cippenham, Slough, Berkshire, SL1 5AP, England

ISBN 0–572–02613-7

Printed in Great Britain by St. Edmundsbury Press, Bury St. Edmunds, Suffolk.

Contents

Introduction

The magic of crystals

Crystals are magical and empowering. The ancient Babylonians first carved magical symbols on bloodstones in order to foretell the future. Indigenous peoples, including the Australian Aborigines and the Native North Americans, have long recognised that stones and crystals are living entities, manifestations of a Great Creative Spirit. The Russian scientist Peter Kirlian discovered that both inorganic and organic gems were surrounded by a radiating energy field that could be captured by special photographic techniques.

The word 'crystal' is rooted in the Greek word *krystallos*, a derivation of *krysos*, meaning 'icy cold', because it was believed that crystals were made from ice so cold it would never melt. Buddhists refer to clear crystal quartz as 'visible nothingness'. The ancient Greeks told that all quartz crystals found on Earth were fragments of the archetypal crystal of truth, dropped by Hercules from Mount Olympus, home of the gods. So whether polished crystal spheres or small divinatory crystals, it is promised in legend that they will never lie to those who consult them.

The Greek philosopher Plato claimed that stars and planets converted decayed and decaying material into the most perfect gemstones, which then came under the rule of those planets and stars, and these planetary associations form part of the divinatory meanings.

Today, divinatory crystals form a focus not only for exploring past influences, present trends and future possibilities as you cast them on a cloth or choose one each day as a guide, but also for healing work and psychic development. The beauty of crystals is that simply by holding or carrying one of the divinatory crystals you become calmer or energised according to the crystal you choose, consciously or unconsciously, as your daily talisman.

Why crystals for women?

Life has never been so complex or challenging for women, who can nowadays fly to the Moon, perform complex microsurgery – and still find time to make a rabbit costume for the playschool performance next day or listen through the night to a friend whose world has suddenly fallen apart. In the 1960s, women were promised they could have it all and be the same as men, and by the turn of the twenty-first century women, old and young, have moved far beyond the confines of the late 1950s when society demanded that little girls washed the teaset while boys rode on the fire engine. But we have also discovered that having it all means doing it all. Surveys have shown that the majority of women, mothers or not, care for the home and for any dependent relatives, that passion is lower on their list of priorities than an early night and that the constant emphasis on dieting and fitness training has caused as many weight problems as it has solved.

There are choices too in lifestyle that would not have been possible even 30 years ago. Whether you are starting out at 16 with the whole world in front of you or are in your eighties and benefiting from the wisdom of maturity and long experience, there are exciting times ahead in the early years of the new century that in a sense give us all a clean slate to write our fortunes anew.

According to a study carried out in the early summer of 1999, a quarter of younger women in the UK have said that they do not want children. When I was 21, not to have an engagement ring on your third finger was akin to social death. But now women are able to choose when – or whether – to enter a permanent relationship and can explore the myriad possibilities of a world that is daily shrinking in terms of communication and travel.

This choice is the key and that is what crystal divination and indeed the other forms of divination in this series are about: taking control, deciding for yourself what would make you happy and not being afraid to change course if other opportunities present themselves or avenues suddenly close or are no longer fulfilling. Crystals will be your best friend when difficulty strikes and there is no doubt that it can: many women today are still constrained by situations not of their making. But crystals are also tools of joy, of dreaming and day-time meditations, and can touch the core of the inner spiritual woman who knows that being alone is not the same as loneliness.

Intuition, the woman's gift

Many women have realised that their strength lies in *not* being exactly like men, that biologists have discovered that the reason for their special gifts of intuitive wisdom and empathy may lie partly in the different neurological connections in the male and female brains. Even the most successful women in worldly terms may find that their natural bodily cycles reflect, not the male solar linear course from A to B, but more the ebbs and flows of the Moon and the tides; by tuning into these natural energy patterns through crystal work, there will be revealed times for maximum input and achievement and others when quiet contemplation and more considered decision-making are better. There is a yearning in many women for a connection with this slower, less tangible level of awareness, based on the need to *be* rather than to *do*.

Can you read the crystals for yourself?

We live in an age of experts. But handing over our destiny, even to the most spiritually evolved clairvoyant or guru, may actually reduce our control over future paths. We all possess intuitive powers: you phone a friend at the same time she dials your number or you *know* when she is in distress, but did not want to bother you. It is the gut feeling that warns you not to trust someone new at work or in your social circle, even though they have the right credentials – and you are invariably right.

It is also the flash of inspiration that turns an issue on its head and cuts through all the indecision and uncertainty, missing out the pages of calculation, and reaching the right answer by a scarcely understood process of induction rather than deduction. Hunches and instincts come more easily to women, precisely because they trust these powers. One female executive said to me: 'The guys have networking: we have intuition', and it is that same intuition that enables us to read our crystals, not to predict a set future, but to explore our potential, the choices before us.

You can of course read crystals for others and if you suggest that they hold the crystals they select, they will sense through their fingertips feelings that will guide them to right action – more of this later.

How does crystal divination work?

Cynics say that any form of divination is pure coincidence and that we read whatever we want into the apparently random selection we make. But the fact is that time after time in hundreds of readings that I have carried out for myself and others, exactly the right crystals are selected, which, when cast, land in a particular area of the cloth in a formation that precisely pinpoints an issue that may only just be surfacing. Or they may suggest a course of action that we would not have thought of when relying purely on logic and the expertise of others.

The psychologist Jung talks about *synchronicity,* or meaningful coincidence, whereby the crystal you select from a bag by touch highlights some inner movement or decision that is soon to be manifest in actual future events; this connection enables you to ride on the crest of the wave rather than being engulfed by its unexpected arrival. Jung locates the source of this knowledge in the collective unconscious, the repository of wisdom derived from all times and places. This well of wisdom that is beyond linear time can be reached through divination, so bypassing the conscious mind. Other psychologists talk of the *tribal voice,* the knowledge and experience of our ancestors that we carry within our genes.

Choosing the right crystal

According to the hypothesis of some psychic researchers, we select the appropriate crystals for our situation by a process of telekinesis, whereby our minds influence the crystals we pick and the way they are thrown. Others have suggested that we have a *second mind*, which is not subject to the constraints of the conscious or rational mind, and that this is the source of all psychic abilities. If we can trust this intuitive mind to come into play in decision-making, then we can increase our potential beyond all belief. Divination is one way of reaching this alternative power-house, which is often called the *female mind*. It is not a question of abandoning deduction, but allowing the inductive mind to combine with what we actually know through analysis and acquired learning.

How can we tell the future?

If we view life as a series of change or nexus points, divination allows us to anticipate these and explore the alternative paths radiating from each one, so that we can decide what steps are to be taken to reach our chosen goal – or perhaps choose to wait and let time heal, or allow events to unfold.

Fate is not fixed, but by our actions and reactions we can narrow down the possibilities it offers, and if we trust our intuition we can glimpse the unexpected factor that can give a whole new spin to the ball game. This is very empowering and can help any woman to cope, no matter how difficult her circumstances.

We may know only too well that we have to take difficult steps, whether to say 'I love you', or 'Goodbye', or to leap into the unknown. So the time you take, borrow or win back from others who make unreasonable demands on your energies – and it can be hard to say 'No', or 'Not now' to those we love – is time well spent. It is your crystal time, precious as you hold each crystal in turn and cast them or meditate upon them. As you enter this gentle, slower world, your psyche can throw off its city suit or protective work clothing, unfold, expand and allow the real essential woman that is you to emerge and evolve.

A special place and time

Ten years ago, when I first explored divination for women, I said it was possible to carry out magic anywhere. Certainly, as a mother of five children who was desperately trying to establish a career in the face of constant tiredness and the feeling of never being able to be still and quiet, magic on the run was all I could manage. And in a sense, I was right, for even if all you have is five minutes with your crystals between appointments or if you regularly arrive home via the supermarket to a week's dirty dishes and a pile of paperwork, then those precious moments do affirm that you, the separate you, still exists and is of importance.

But over the years, I have come to realise that work expands to fit the time available and that work colleagues or family members, however loving, encroach on and erode that separate person. I have also learned that the gesture of creating a special place and time for divination and self-development helps to define these limits of self and put markers between the everyday world and this vital, separate part of your life. So make yourself a magical area – it may be no more than a shelf or table on which you keep scented candles, flowers, crystals, shells – considered in earlier times to be a symbol of the Mother Goddess – and small treasures you bring back from holidays or special days out. You may choose a goddess statue from a tradition that appeals to you or a model or picture of an animal that embodies the powers that you admire or feel you symbolically share.

But above all it is a place for your crystals, both your divinatory ones and any special ones you may choose or be given as presents: perhaps a large piece of unpolished rose quartz or amethyst for harmony, clear crystal inclusions or a pointed quartz crystal as your energising and empowering wand, in the tradition of those fairy godmothers of pre-Christian times, the powerful female pagan deities of love, the Moon and the hunt. You might buy a golden citrine still in the rock to serve as a focus for clear communication, or a piece of dark obsidian or smoky quartz which, when you hold it up to the light, will show you the promises of a brighter tomorrow, a reminder that after every ending comes a new beginning and after the darkness there is always the dawn.

If you can set aside a special corner or room for your divinatory work where the sunlight will shed rainbows and the moonbeams or the light of a candle can bring a soft translucence to your crystals, you are already claiming back personal space in the most spiritual sense, whether you live in a shared flat or family home. If you live alone, make this area separate from your working and living environment.

You can invite close friends, partners or even children into this space and they too can absorb some of the tranquillity and power that it will accumulate as you dream, meditate and work with your crystals. Our ancestors made the hearth their sacred focus and refuge, and at night, when everyone was in bed, several generations of women would sit in companionable silence in a half-trance state, seeing pictures in the embers and watching the candlelight flickering against the walls.

Treasure these special moments and consciously push away the list of chores and challenges that belong to tomorrow. If the weather is fine, you may wish to transfer your special place out of doors, perhaps to a corner of the garden sheltered by bushes, or a summer house, or even a balcony. You can use a piece of wood supported on bricks or a tree trunk for your work space, or, like our forebears, choose a large rock on which to set your crystals and candles.

Try also to set aside a special time each day for your crystals. This may not always be easy, given the multiplicity of roles that most women are expected to play nowadays. But you should not feel that taking an hour or so out for yourself is an act of pure selfishness. Just a short time spent working with your crystals, concentrating on your own self, and thinking your own thoughts, will pay dividends for you and those around you, restoring your equilibrium, refreshing your mind and preparing you for whatever tasks you may have ahead.

To help you, I have laid out this book in days, instead of chapters, each one containing just enough information for one session with your stones. If you stick to the format, it should take you just a month to read. Of course, you do not have to be ruled by your crystals, so there will be days when you have more time, and will read more – and there may be others when you miss out altogether.

But whenever and wherever you work with your crystals, you will be able to make it a time and place of peace, knowledge, enjoyment and fulfilment.

Divinatory crystals

The divination system is based on 20 crystals in ten colours, two different stones of each colour. If you can afford only one of each colour, you can still get very accurate readings – buy one of the crystals in the colour section marked with an asterisk (*) and use the relevant meaning for divination, either creative or receptive according to the stone chosen.

Though colour is important in crystal divination, each crystal has its own special energies. What is more, crystal work is essentially personal and each of us interacts with crystals in our own unique way. Though I have listed throughout the book the traditional magical, astrological and healing associations of various crystals, crystal wisdom is innate in us all and so the system here is a template from which you will create your own magic.

Creative and receptive stones

Each colour is represented by two kinds of stones: one is bright and richly coloured and may be either opaque (so that you cannot see through it) or transparent and sparkling. The other is gentler in hue, sometimes transparent or semi-transparent and sometimes opaque; it will have a delicate shade, and may be matt like a pebble or translucent, softly reflecting the light.

All crystals contain two complementary forces: the first is a creative, positive, masculine, physical and logical energy, the *yang* of the Chinese spiritual systems, Sky or Air and Fire energies, the power of the Sun. The second is a receptive, feminine, spiritual and intuitive power, negative only in the sense of an opposing electrical charge, the *yin* energies, corresponding to Earth and Water, the power of the Moon. Both are equally essential. This duality mirrors our own composition. We all possess a masculine and a feminine side (Jung's *animus* and *anima*), and have both a creative, energising impetus and a nurturing, receptive aspect to our nature.

Crystals, like people, tend to have more of one type of energy than the other and so we can categorise stones as mainly either *creative* or *receptive*, for the purpose of divination, healing and magic. Whether you cast the creative or receptive aspect of the colour in divination can suggest whether you should act and be assertive, or wait and perhaps be prepared to compromise. When healing, a creative stone will add empowering energy and a receptive stone will remove pain or anxiety.

But there are no rigid categories, so you need to handle each crystal and *feel* whether it is empowering or soothing for you. As long as one shade and intensity of any one colour represents for you the creative and the other the receptive element, the system will work. Indeed, the beauty of crystals is that your energising stones will become more positive as you use them and the receptive stones gentler and more harmonious. Select crystals that are round and smooth, but sufficiently flat to lie on a cloth when cast. They should be about the size of a large coin.

A basic crystal list

Some stones are found in a variety of colours. Where this is the case, the core meaning is given either the first time it is mentioned or for the core stone of the type. Any extra or different properties are listed under the relevant colour.

Read through the list and mark any stones that seem especially relevant to your life. You can refer to the list when you buy your crystals.

Creative white*

- **Crystal quartz:** Transparent or semi-transparent (also in a variety of colours; less commonly cloudy or opaque). Recognised in all times and cultures as a powerful transmitter of physical and psychic energies, clear crystal quartz will amplify the energies of the user, drawing out negative energies and sending positive ones in their place. A powerful focus for divination or meditation, linking the user with the Higher Self and realms of consciousness.

Fluorite: Also red, yellow, green, blue and purple. Denotes objectivity and change. Clears away stagnation, preparing the way for new experiences; promotes psychic awareness and amplifies other crystals.

Zircon: Colourless in its natural form. Spiritual awareness, intuition and contact with other dimensions and the Life Force; relieves depression, insomnia and nightmares.

Receptive white

Milky/snow quartz: Opaque, soothing, bringing balance and slower, gentler energies to restore hope after sorrow or loss. It melts away lingering doubts and offers the gradual restoration of enthusiasm. A wise stone, tempered by experience.

Moonstone or selenite: Translucent, also fawn, pink, yellow, occasionally blue sheen. Moonstone is believed to absorb the powers of the Moon, becoming deeper in colour, more translucent and more powerful for healing as the Moon waxes until it becomes a Full Moon. As the Moon wanes, so the moonstone becomes paler and less potent.

Moonstone is the stone of travellers, especially by night or on the sea, whose tides the Moon rules. It is associated with women and with unconscious powers of ancient knowledge. Moonstone is a stone of gardening and of fertility, both in plants and in women. Moonstones sometimes contain what appear to be fossilised insects but are in fact inner cleavages; a source of inner wisdom and hidden treasures of our psyche, encouraging sensitivity, clairvoyance and intuition.

Mother of pearl: An organic gem, formed from the glossy pearly inside of an oyster shell; oval stones as well as beads are available, although this is not a stone as such. Carries the peaceful healing energy of the sea; soothes extremes of emotions, protects against over-sensitivity. Strengthens connections between mothers and children. Excellent for meditation, psychometry (gaining impressions by holding it) and scrying (gazing into the stone).

Creative black

Hematite: Silver-grey metallic brilliance. A powerful earthing and protective stone that clears indecision, aids concentration, improves memory and helps all forms of study and areas where attention to detail is vital. Builds confidence, will-power and self-esteem and strengthens courage; acts as a shield against physical and emotional hostility and aids astral projection.

Jasper: Black jasper was used as a touchstone to identify pure gold and so represents discrimination and the need to preserve what is of worth. It is protective against all negative sources, especially the user's own repressed feelings, and is good for absorbing anger. (See also Red jasper, page 20).

Jet: An organic gem, jet is fossilised wood that has been turned into a dense form of coal, and like amber is of great antiquity. It is sacred to Cybele, mother of the gods in classical mythology. Since the Bronze Age, jet from Yorkshire has been used for ornaments and jewellery.

Like amber, jet is used as a doorway into other dimensions, especially the past, and in divination for increasing psychic powers generally.

Receptive black*

Dark-banded agate: Grounding, balance and stability, security, acceptance of self and others as they are; emotional and physical balance. Banded agates are the true agates in geological terms and tend to be receptive, while the single colours are creative.

In Roman times agates were specially prized stones and the Romans produced beautiful agate cameos by using the many different coloured layers. Agates were once used in Asia for scrying, as we do with our present-day crystal balls, and throughout the world as amulets. They are therefore protective stones and should be worn or carried in times of potential hostility.

Obsidian (Apache's tears): I used to regard this as a creative stone, but over the years have come to see that its courage is gentle and based on endurance. Legend has it that a group of Apaches in Arizona were ambushed by soldiers; many were killed and the rest threw themselves over a cliff, rather than be taken. The women and maidens of the tribe wept at the base of the cliff for a whole Moon cycle and their tears became embedded within obsidian crystals. Those who carry this form of obsidian will never, it is said, know deep sorrow. When you hold this crystal to the light, you can see new hope and life glimmering.

Obsidian eases and releases physical and mental pain, loss, sadness and anger, to allow the user to move forward. It is a stone of acceptance of life as it is.

Smoky quartz: Dark grey, semi-transparent/opaque, also brown. Smoky quartz is traditionally associated with removing negative influences on the user, both by improving physical health and in galvanising our shadow side. It transforms anger and resentment into positive action, rather than denying negative feelings or projecting them on to others; the stone of survival instincts, providing the power to endure and surmount difficult odds.

Creative red*

Blood agate: Rich and glowing, offers courage to turn obstacles into challenges; the crystal of noble sacrifice and the crusader.

Carnelian: Translucent, also yellow, orange and red, occasionally brown. The word carnelian comes from the Latin for flesh. It was regarded as the stone of courage and self-confidence, of leaders and would-be leaders, when worn around the neck or in a ring. In the Middle Ages, carnelian talismans were engraved with symbols of classical heroes and heroines to give a home protection against storms, lightning and fire.

Carnelian strengthens creativity, brings abundance to all aspects of life, repels envy in others and enhances confidence, courage, initiative, assertiveness and all positive emotions. A catalyst for change.

In the ancient Eastern world, carnelian was used as an aid to astral travel – a use that has continued.

Garnet: Also green, orange and colourless. A protective stone, used by Eastern European peoples against illness, night phantoms and all forms of manifest evil, including the mythical vampire. In mediaeval times, garnets were engraved with a lion's head to ensure health and safe travel; it is still regarded as a stone for travellers, especially as a safeguard against attack. It stimulates action and passion and increases will-power, stamina, confidence, self-esteem and persistence as well as imagination.

Red jasper: Opaque, also multi-coloured with single colours as yellow, orange, brown, black (see page 18), green, sometimes found as petrified wood.

From early times, jasper has been used for official seals and, like agate, jasper was used in carvings, mosaics and cameos because of its variety of colours. Jasper, like jade, is associated with rain rituals – the Native North American name for the stone was 'rain-bringer'.

Jasper acts as a defence against hostility and brings stability and courage under difficulty. It is thus a powerful protective stone, but also offers the stamina to initiate necessary change.

Receptive red

Banded agate: Opaque with more muted reddish-brown and pink colouring than the blood agate. Known as the earth rainbow for making practical wishes come true. Resistance to any who would override your needs and rights, but in a measured way, rather than blind anger. See also Dark-banded agate (page 18).

Calcite: Transparent or semi-transparent pale red (also milky yellow, peach, green, white or clear crystals). Assists in astral projection; balances yang and yin, masculine and feminine energies, assertive and accepting qualities in people. Needs care in handling as it can be brittle. Buy a polished stone. A valuable stone in healing as well as divination as it prevents excesses and lessens obsessions and addictive habits.

Fluorite: Transparent, in all colours of the rainbow. A powerful harmoniser, promotes physical and emotional clarity and wider perspective. If in doubt, buy a fluorite for a steady release of restorative and yet calming energies. Good for hyperactivity and restlessness in children and adults alike. Takes the heat out of confrontations.

Creative orange*

Amber: Yellow and golden brown. Fossilised tree resin, usually about 50 million years old, and may contain remains of plants, insects and even lizards. According to Chinese tradition, the souls of tigers pass into amber when they die and so it is a gem of courage. It is also said to contain the power of many suns. Good for all past life work and astral projection. A stone of joy, wisdom and perspective. Its popular name, the honey stone, indicates its warming, integrating qualities and so it enables the user to see the present as part of a greater pattern. Favours the long-term perspective and solution, and is good for fidelity.

Carnelian: Tempers courage and impetus for change with the reality principle and an awareness of the implications of action. See also Red carnelian, page 19.

Jasper: Optimism, faith in one's own ability to win through. A stone of reliability, controlled effort and persistence. See also Red jasper, page 20.

Receptive orange

Banded agate: Muted orange. The assimilator and sifter of truth and stone of integrity. Known sometimes as 'the stone of the desert', it offers assurance that to persevere is to win through. See also Dark-banded agate, page 18.

Calcite: Uplifting, brings joy and good humour, faith in human nature and an overriding but quiet optimism. See also Red calcite, page 20.

Beryl: Also golden brown, blue and pink. A crystal of the Sun, it gently increases confidence, will-power and visualisation abilities. A protective crystal, it counteracts exhaustion, depression, fear and resentment and is helpful in difficult situations or where there are many factors to assimilate. Some see this as a creative stone, but it is more a stone of the morning or evening rather than the noonday Sun. The stone of the unchanging inner woman.

Creative yellow*

Citrine: Clear, sparkling yellow. Promotes mental and emotional clarity; good for problem-solving, improving long- and short-term memory and will-power and inspiring optimism, self-confidence and self-discipline; reduces anxiety and depression. Good for removing mental and physical energy blockages.

Jasper: Enables the user to take what is of worth from a situation, and protects against jealousy and the build-up of resentment. Encourages grounding and acceptance of others and life as they really are. See also Red jasper, page 20.

Topaz: Golden, clear and sparkling (also pink, pale blue, orange or brown). The word topaz means 'fire' in Sanskrit. It increases power with the Moon, being at its greatest potency at the time of the Full Moon. Perhaps because of this, topaz was said to give protection against nightmares and night terrors as well as violent emotion. Psychically, it is a stone of astral travel and according to the belief of the ancient Easterns confers invisibility on its wearer; promotes mental clarity, focused thinking and abstract reasoning, confidence, will-power and stamina; helps in letting go of the past, enhances creativity.

Zircon: A stone of mental and physical clarity, good for communication of all kinds and for clearing misunderstandings. See also Colourless zircon, page 17.

Receptive yellow

Calcite: Moderates the sharpness of yellow stones with gentle optimism and an awareness of the need for communication that does not diminish the recipient. See also Red calcite, page 20.

Fluorite: Encourages clear focus, co-operation and working with others in formal groups or organisations. A stone of inner beauty and worth. See also Red fluorite, page 21.

Rutilated quartz: Clear quartz with metallic, golden rutile (also sometimes brown). Rutilated quartz was created, according to legend, when angels froze the water of the heavens; it is also said that guardian angels dwell in rutilated quartz, offering protection and wise counsel to users.

The stone of inner wisdom and undeveloped potential, rutilated quartz is said to heal all inner ills, amplifying healing energy and thoughts and breaking destructive patterns of behaviour.

Creative green

Aventurine: Translucent dark or light green quartz. Encourages mental clarity, joy and a positive attitude, and heals emotional pain and fears. It is a stone of travelling in hope, whether physically or mentally, and of emotional regeneration.

Bloodstone: Opaque, mottled green and red. A stone of courage. Links the user with higher states of consciousness. The red spots were, according to legend, formed from the blood of Christ as it fell on green jasper at the crucifixion and so it is traditionally used in icons and religious carvings. Protects against jealousy, increases empathy with others' difficulties, soothes bad dreams.

Cat's eye: Clear, green or green/brown (can also be golden yellow). There are several kinds, but all have an opalescence that resembles a cat's eye and so the stone is excellent for promoting keen vision, both physical and inner. Promotes abundance, both material and spiritual, and confidence. A cat's eye is sometimes left in a jar of money to increase prosperity. Avoid those that have been artificially irradiated.

Malachite: Green with black stripes. A purifier and energiser, replacing negativity with positive energies; soothes physical hurt and the pain caused by harsh or critical words; concentrates psychic vision, especially in meditation.

Receptive green*

Amazonite: Opaque, light blue/turquoise. Gentle, calming, integrates different aspects of mind, body and spirit, encourages self-expression and artistic creativity. Limits self-damaging behaviour; improves self-worth and self-confidence.

Chrysoprase: Translucent bright or apple green. Encourages flexibility in the face of problems, wisdom, generosity and self-confidence, and alleviates depression, self-doubts and extreme emotional swings. Place on the heart or neck to promote meditation.

Jade: Many shades of green, opaque to translucent. A stone for health, prosperity and long life; in the Orient, jade was associated with reincarnation – a piece of jade was placed on the eyelids or in the mouth of the dead to ensure the spirit would return for another life on earth. Jade bowls were used to energise food with the life force. In China, jade is used as a talisman, carved in the shape of a butterfly, to attract love. It is also given as a love token to those who are the object of love, and on the occasion of a formal betrothal. Jade pendants are worn by oriental children to ward off illness and harm.

Jade, like rose quartz and coral, is a stone for children because of its gentleness. It offers wisdom, quiet courage, emotional balance, stamina, altruism, love, fidelity, peace, humility and generosity, and connects the user with earth energies.

Moss agate: Really colourless, but contains a profusion of tree-like growths of muted green minerals. Agates were sacred to the gods of vegetation and even today the moss agate is especially associated with gardening and all kinds of growth, and with prosperity. See also Dark-banded agate, page 18.

Creative blue*

Azurite: Solid deep blue, sometimes flecked with paler blue, also blue-purple. Amplifies innate healing abilities; good for assertiveness, clear communication, decision-making, alertness and creativity. Promotes access to psychic awareness and past lives and the experience of the collective wisdom of mankind. Reduces depression and anger.

Falcon's eye/hawk's eye: Blue and chatoyant, reflecting light in a wavy band (also green). Reveals the reality of situations, and gives wider perspective and focus, and sharpened perception for mental and spiritual growth. A stone of courage and determination. Like the hawk and falcon, if you aim high and focus on a specific goal, you will succeed.

Howzite: The version that is dyed blue is a good substitute for the more expensive turquoise listed below and takes on its properties. A powerful stone for gaining power over your own emotions.

Laboradite: Metallic, iridescent, varied bluey-green hues from quite rich to more subtle (sometimes yellow). Brings out unique talents for the good of others; encourages originality, diversity and independent action. Some people regard it as a receptive stone in its softer hues, but it is a stone of inner strength.

Turquoise: Opaque, light blue/blue-green. Mined by the Egyptians in Sinai more than 6,000 years ago, turquoise and its imitations have been discovered in graves from around 4000 BC.

Known as a male stone of power in Central America because it could only be worn by warriors, turquoise is regarded as a Sky stone, a manifestation of the Source of Creation, and for this reason it can offer women the strength to fulfil ambitions and fight inertia in others. A protective stone, turquoise absorbs all negative forces. It endows wisdom on those who wear it and increases psychic communication.

Receptive blue

Aquamarine: Clear light blue, blue-green to dark blue. The name means 'water of the sea' in Latin and has traditionally been the stone of sailors and fishermen, inducing mental clarity, spiritual inspiration, creativity, communication, self-awareness, clear communication and confidence. A form of beryl (see page 21) and so its powers are mitigated by gentleness and altruism. Links with the ebbs and flow of the female monthly and life cycle.

Blue lace agate: Translucent, pale blue, this crystal calms strong emotions, creating a sense of peace and encouraging patience, especially with children and in situations that cannot be changed. A stone of compromise and speaking truthfully but with kindness.

Celestite: Semi-transparent or transparent, light-blue cluster crystals (also white). Called 'the crystal of the angels'. Gentle, slows racing thoughts. Connects with spiritual nature, encourages creativity. Worth seeking out as a suitable divinatory stone as it is a crystal that links with higher consciousness, the Higher Self, angelic or spirit guides.

Moonstone: The blue moonstone is rare and said only to be formed on the 'Blue Moon' when there is more than one Full Moon in a month; in Asia the belief is that the best ones are washed up on the shore when the Sun and Moon are in a certain harmonious relationship which only occurs every 21 years – hence the saying 'Once in a blue moon'. For dreams, intuition and romance and for valuing every moment of joy and taking every opportunity for new experience. See also White moonstone, page 17.

Creative purple

Lapis lazuli/lazurite: Opaque, purple flecked with iron pyrites, fool's gold (also deep blue). Known as 'the eye of wisdom', the stone of the gods, lapis lazuli jewellery is mentioned as having healing powers in an ancient Egyptian papyrus written over 3,000 years ago. The Sumerians believed it contained the souls of their gods and goddesses and as such would endow them with magical powers.

Because of its association with the wisdom of higher powers, lapis lazuli is considered powerful in aiding psychic awareness and combining unconscious wisdom with the conscious powers of the mind; it encourages creative expression, especially through writing, oratory and profound dreams. A stone to help you make the right decisions.

Sodalite: Many shades of purple – deep indigo with white being the most common (also deep blue). Denotes communication, both spoken and written; the stone of writers and poets; promotes logical thinking, creativity, courage, harmony, idealism and altruism; alleviates subconscious guilt and fears; offers protection from negative energies of all kinds. Good for meditation.

Sugilite: Opaque rich purple (also pink). Absorbs negativity from the wearer or user's aura and replaces it with positive energies. Removes emotional blocks and reduces stress levels. Placed on the forehead, it alleviates depression and feelings of worthlessness or despair; integrates the left and right hemispheres of the brain, producing a mixture of reason and intuitive thought.

Receptive purple*

Amethyst: From pale lilac and lavender to deep purple, translucent, semi-transparent and transparent, sometimes flecked with white. One of the most effective stones of healing, amethyst assists spiritual and psychic development while keeping connection with the Earth, enhancing creativity, courage and intuition. Egyptian soldiers wore amethyst in battle so that they would not panic in dangerous situations. Helps communication, especially in spiritual matters, and fights all forms of excess and compulsion. For this reason, it was used by the ancient Greeks and Romans for drinking goblets.

Fluorite: Deep purple. Lavender promotes a sense of inner peace, serenity and harmony with nature and the life force. In clusters, it lowers stress levels caused by work or life in general and can be placed either in the workplace or home to absorb negativity and hyperactivity of others. Links with other dimensions. See also Clear fluorite, page 17.

Kunzite: Transparent (also pink). A potent stone, sometimes known as 'the woman's stone', because of its ability to soothe all female disorders; increases compassion and the ability to give unconditional love. Good for overcoming compulsive behaviour and addictions; restores confidence and reduces depression, extreme mood swings and stress; opens psychic and spiritual channels for divination and healing.

Creative pink

Coral: A protective opaque organic gem (also in red and orange). Coral has been a children's stone from the time of the ancient Greeks, when Plato wrote that it should be hung around children's necks to prevent them falling. Coral was nailed to ships' masts to protect them from storms. Increases sensitivity and compassion and protects the user from fears and anxieties, especially those left from the past.

Rhodonite: Opaque pink with black inclusions. Offers emotional support. Gives courage to take the next step towards happiness or freedom; effective for mantras, chanting, positive affirmations and for clairaudience.

Rhodochrosite: Opaque to clear pink, sometimes salmon pink, banded with paler colour. A stone of gradual change, providing the confidence to make alterations in lifestyle. Enables major changes to be made without stress. Has stronger and more intense energies than rose quartz (see below); its vibrant powers assist the ability to give and receive love. Strengthens identity and relieves loneliness, grief and insecurity and unresolved childhood issues.

Sugilite: Gentle inspirations, gives the ability to know instinctively how best to respond in sensitive situations. The stone of tact. See also Purple sugilite, page 27.

Receptive pink*

Rose quartz: Translucent to clear pink, like amethyst, an excellent stone for all forms of healing; known as 'the children's stone' because it is so gentle in soothing away childhood ills and sorrows, but is equally effective with troubled adults. Promotes family love and friendship, brings peace, forgiveness and the mending of quarrels and emotional harmony; heals emotional wounds, heartbreak, grief, stress, fear, lack of confidence, resentment and anger; good for alleviating sorrows left from childhood. A stone for quiet and regular sleep patterns.

Kunzite: A wonderful stone for girls entering puberty, for all problems concerning fertility and for tired mothers. See also Purple kunzite, page 27.

Morganite/Pink beryl: Clear/soft pink (also violet), translucent to clear. Encourages compassion, empathy and patience. Guides the user to the highest standards of thought and action. Protective. See also Beryl, page 21.

Tourmaline: Also black, blue, green, watermelon striated, clear/semi-transparent gem. Pink tourmaline endows love, of self and others, and increases insight and perception, both physical and emotional; removes old sorrows and redundant regrets; balances the natural desire for peace with necessary assertiveness for well-being. Promotes sympathy and friendship. It is worth seeking a good divinatory stone, especially if you face continuing potential disharmony in your life.

Creative brown

Agate: Brown or tawny for business acumen and for practical and financial security; the crystal of firm foundations in every way. Keeps you safe from the wheeling and dealing of the less scrupulous. See also Blood agate, page 19.

Brown amber: Enables the user to take a long-term perspective on money or practical worries. Slows down any frantic activity with a more measured approach. See also Amber, page 21.

Brown jasper: Sharpens the five senses and offers a stable base in turbulent times; good to use after divination or meditation to restore the everyday world without losing the insights gained. See also Red jasper, page 20.

Tiger's eye: Yellow-gold and brown stripes, chatoyant (also burgundy stripes). The stone of independence, combining the powers of the Earth with the deep instinctive ability to survive life's challenges. Throughout the ages, tiger's eye has been a talisman against the evil eye. Roman soldiers would wear engraved stones as protection from death and wounding. Tiger's eye is associated with practical aspects of life and enhances health in the five senses. Above all, it is a stone of balance, offering a sense of perspective and the ability to see other people's points of view, separating thoughts from feelings and desires from need; encourages strong identity and decision-making.

Receptive brown*

Desert rose: An opaque, light brown, rough-textured stone. Almost like a nut with glints of quartz. Clarifies thinking and practical planning, sharpens perceptions. Grounding; calms racing thoughts; enables the mind to sort out priorities and step off the treadmill of life. A stone of hidden treasures and gradually unfolding spirituality that can co-exist with the everyday world.

Leopardskin/snakeskin jasper: Mottled. Encourages the shedding of what is redundant. Brings what one needs, rather than what one wants. Some people regard this stone as creative, but I feel that the energies involve accepting a necessary stage of life. It does, however, promise that new life will come when the time is right – a new spring after a winter of doubt. See also Red jasper, page 20.

DAY 2
Choosing your divinatory crystals

This is a very special day, so, if possible, spend the whole day alone or with a friend or family member who will not become impatient as you slow your pace of life and put yourself first. Even the most materially successful woman can worry about making others happy, but today it is your happiness that is the focus. If you feel in harmony with the world, anything is possible, so enjoy the company of your very best friend: yourself. Take along this book or a photocopy of the list of crystals I suggested in the previous chapter.

You can buy your crystals by mail order (I have suggested some useful addresses at the back of this book), but it is better to spend time handling a variety of crystals in each colour and kind, as each will *feel* different. In the ten years since I first wrote about this subject, crystals have become widely available, not only in New Age shops and in mineral stores, but in gift shops, in holiday resorts, museums and theme parks. You may wish to choose crystals that are not on the list, in which case use one of the books listed on page 154 to find out about the magical and healing properties of the crystals you select.

If possible, don't do any other shopping; when you have selected your crystals, spend the rest of the day in any way *you* enjoy, whether visiting an old building or a museum, walking down by the river, going to a place you have always wanted to visit or exploring a craft market, hunting for just the right place for lunch or tea. In this way, the crystals are from the beginning naturally imbued with your essence at its most peaceful and happy.

Choose a drawstring bag large enough to keep your crystals, one that embodies your dream self, made of an Oriental or a delicate

Victorian flower fabric. If you prefer, you can buy fabric to sew one and in the manner of our ancestors, endow each stitch with a wish or empowerment.

Recently I found myself with a rare day to spare between broadcasts in Sheffield and I took a bus out to the Derbyshire Dales, to Bakewell, a town I had wanted to visit for more than 30 years. Although I am used to travelling extensively, it was quite frightening as well as exhilarating to answer the question 'What do I *want* to do?' and to push away the anxieties about the thousand and one tasks I needed to fulfil. It was a wonderful day and I bought some new crystals which, when I use them, recall the pleasure of stepping off the treadmill and just walking through the rain by the river.

Finding crystals

There is something very magical about finding, as opposed to buying, crystals and stones, and this has become a feature of my family outings to the shore or countryside. If you pick up a piece of quartz from the beach or hillside and hold it to the sunlight, you may see light glinting through it. Even a brown or black opaque stone has a story and may reveal in quiet moments impressions of far-off lands and times where it originated.

You may also receive crystals as gifts, once people know of your interest. Crystals given in love and friendship are especially potent. Later in the book I suggest ways of adding these crystals to your basic divinatory set. But for now, keep these extra crystals in your special place and spend time with them, gazing within them and letting impressions flow.

Beginning crystal magic

Give yourself a special evening too. If it's not possible to fit it all into one day, do it tomorrow. The 'days' of this book are merely for guidance and you may go a whole week without having time to learn anything new, or have a surge and cover three days in one.

First, have a bath using a few drops of an essential oil that releases your natural psychic awareness, for example, sandalwood, geranium or rose.

Light a circle of purple candles, scented with lavender for evoking your inner wisdom, and sit in what is or will become your special place.

Tip all your crystals on the table or floor. As you do so, try to recapture the excitement of those childhood days when you tipped out a button box and wove stories about the pearl or rhinestone ones, imagining you danced at balls with a handsome prince. Handsome princes are in short supply nowadays and those that do exist usually have alimony suits from ex-princesses or will leave you alone for hours while they blast the heads off furry animals in chilly Scottish glens. Still, the dreams we weave now may be different from those girlish ones, but the principle is the same.

Touch your crystals one by one and let images form, both from your inner world of dreams as you did as a child and from the stones themselves. This is called psychometry, the ability to receive impressions by touch, whether a sight, a sound or even a fragrance, for it is said that every rock and crystal contains impressions of the past. This imaging process uses the visual parts of the brain, situated in the right hemisphere. This ability is readily accessed by children, but can fall into disuse as we verbalise and categorise all experience in reality. Both have a place in divination, but the ability to see pictures as you cast and touch the stones in readings, enables you to move beyond set meanings and to use the stones as a focus for intuitive images.

Colin Wilson, perhaps the best-known writer on the paranormal, once said that there are no entirely accurate forms of divination *per se* – the vision lies in the interpreter. If you find psychometry difficult at first, imagine you are telling a child a story about the crystal, seeing within each a living essence, whose story gradually unfolds. Closing your eyes and relying purely on touch also helps.

Later you will select a crystal each day to act as a guide and talisman and any time you spend either in the morning or evening, weaving ever-changing stories around it, will enable you to access deep wisdom from the collective store of mankind that has passed to us in myth and legend, our spiritual history.

DAY 3
Cleansing and empowering your crystals

Cleansing your crystals

Before charging your crystals with power, you may wish to cleanse them, to remove all the energies (not necessarily negative) of those who have prepared, packed and sold the stones. However, this is not essential unless a stone does not 'feel' right.

You will also need to cleanse your crystals regularly to clear them of negative energy after carrying out a number of readings, especially if you have been carrying out readings for others who may have unconsciously projected their worries and frustrations.

Cleansing using the forces of nature

Arrange your stones clockwise in a circle in an approximation of a rainbow formation, beginning with creative white, the source of light and pure energy, followed by receptive white, then creative and receptive red, orange, yellow, green, blue and purple. Place your pink crystals after the receptive purple, then the brown, ending the circle with receptive black (this is not strictly a colour, but an absence of colour, the gentle darkness that absorbs all colours in rest and tranquillity). Allow the stones to touch gently.

Leave your crystal circle in sunlight and moonlight for 24 hours or in a rainstorm, ensuring that the rain does not touch the ground before it cleanses the crystals.

Alternatively, create the crystal circle on the surface of the soil in a pot of herbs that are associated with general healing, for example lavender, sage or rosemary, so that the circle surrounds the plant. Leave it for 24 hours and, if necessary, wash off any soil from individual crystals with running water.

Cleansing using other crystals

Place a large uncut piece of amethyst in the centre of the circle to absorb negativity. Afterwards soak the amethyst and a large piece of unpolished crystal quartz together for 24 hours in a glass container of rainwater (again make sure that it has not touched the ground in its collection) to restore the energies of the amethyst.

If acid rain is a problem in your region, add a few drops of a flower essence that calms and protects, for example Dr Bach's Agrimony or Goatbeard from the Pacific Flower Essence Remedies, or Coconut Palm from the African and Amazonian Essences. You can also use a dropper to sprinkle your crystal circle with flower essences, if you are using the rain cleansing method described on page 35.

Empowering your crystals for divination and healing

After you have cleansed a crystal, you can charge it with power for healing, magic and divination. These processes are very close and merge into one quite spontaneously after you have worked with your crystals for a few weeks. When you carry out a reading for yourself or others, restorative energies will be transmitted to the questioner and needs or dreams that are expressed through the stones will become empowerments, through the increased power of the crystals combined with your own naturally evolving psychic abilities.

You will need to recharge your crystals with energy after you have used them for a while or after cleansing them from negativity.

Empowering using a crystal pendulum

You can empower your crystals using a crystal pendulum. Recreate your rainbow crystal circle. Hold a clear crystal pendulum in the centre of the circle of crystals and pass the pendulum over it nine times in slow, ever-increasing clockwise circles, seeing with each cycle glowing energies emanating from the pendulum and entering each crystal in turn.

Keep your pendulum well charged and positive for future empowerments by running it under cold clear water and then leaving it in water steeped with rose petals over which a cleansing incense such as pine or cedar and a white candle flame have been passed.

Empowering using the ancient elements

This is the oldest method of dedicating and empowering crystals. From classical times until the reign of the Tudors, the four elements – Earth, Air, Fire and Water – were considered to be the basic building blocks of all life. Now the periodic table of the elements has replaced this belief but the ancient elements are still symbolically important, and like the ancients we still describe people as 'earthy', 'fiery', 'wet' or 'airy' when speaking of their psychological or physical characteristics. It was believed that from these four elements a fifth – sometimes called *ether* or *akasha* – was synthesised.

✢ Sprinkle the crystal circle with a few grains of salt, beginning at the symbolic north of the circle (the 12 o'clock position), to represent the Earth element. As you do so, make a personal Earth empowerment, repeating as a mantra, for example

Mother Earth, give wisdom birth.

✢ Next, describe circles with two sticks of incense, first frankincense or rosemary for the Sun, held in your right hand, nine times clockwise and then jasmine or sandalwood for the Moon, held in the left hand, nine times anti-clockwise, around the outside of the crystal circle; for each begin in the symbolic east, (the three o'clock position). This represents the Air element. As you do so, make an Air empowerment, repeating as a mantra, for example:

Father Air, your vision share.

✢ Using a broad-based holder so that hot wax does not drip, begin in the symbolic south (the six o'clock position) and circle your crystals nine times clockwise, with a gold or orange candle for the element of Fire. Repeat as a mantra something like:

Brother Fire, my words inspire.

✢ Finally sprinkle your circle of crystals with pure water, scented with roses or rose or lavender essential oil, nine times clockwise, beginning in the symbolic west (the nine o'clock position) for the Water element, speaking a mantra such as:

Sister Water last of all, gentle love upon me fall.

DAY 4
White crystals

White is the only colour to have two planetary rulers, one for each aspect, creative and receptive, since it is the synthesis of all other colours. White crystals embody new beginnings, energy and creative power.

Take your two white crystals from the bag and hold the clear stone in your right hand, for left-brain logic, reasoning and verbal communication powers, and your gentler white stone in your left hand, for right-brain intuition, visual imaging and inspirational powers. The left side of the brain controls the right hand and vice versa, and together they offer the integration of reason and intuition, Sun and Moon. And so your white crystals that integrate solar and lunar powers are in any reading a promise that joy will be yours, whether immediately or more gradually over a period of days, weeks or even months, if you accept the challenges and opportunities that are coming into your life. They are the stones of initiation and of innovation.

Reading white crystals

If you are using only one white crystal, choose the creative form.

Creative white

Creative white crystals, whether a crystal quartz, a zircon, fluorite or other clear white stone, represent the pure Life Force, the Crown *chakra* or the psychic energy centre at the top of the head (more of this later) and Kether, the Crown in the Hebrew mystical system, the Kabbalah. This is the brilliance of pure sunlight and is ruled by the Sun.

But it is not at all a male power – indeed some of the solar deities, especially of indigenous peoples, were female. For example Sol (or Sunna) of the Norse tradition rode her Sun chariot drawn by the horses, Aarvak (the early-waker) and Alavin (the rapid-goer), with a golden shield to protect them from the heat of the Sun. In ancient Japan, the chief deity or kami (essence of divinity) was Amaterasu Omigami, the Sun Goddess. All natural phenomena were seen as manifestations, of her divinity. Her name means 'Great August Spirit Shining in Heaven' but she is also called Shinmet, 'Divine Radiance' – and O-hiru-me-no-muchi – 'Great Female Possessor of Noon'.

Like the Sun, creative white crystals represent pure energy, the *animus* or *yang* energy that women need to succeed in important aspects of their life; they are crystals of individuality and pure potential.

Creative white stones offer the impetus that enables a plane to take off from the tarmac, they mirror the peak experience when all the pieces of the your life momentarily fit together – 'sudden in a shaft of sunlight', as T.S. Eliot put it in *The Four Quartets* – and the way ahead becomes clear.

When a creative white crystal appears in a reading you know, whatever your age or lifestyle, it is time for an exciting new beginning, when you can develop your talents, or fulfil your ambitions whether they are to grow beautiful sunflowers or be president of a merchant bank. Joy, confidence and enthusiasm abound and you can soar high.

Seize the moment, focus on the here and now that ultimately frees us from past and, as the *I Ching* says, 'Be as the sun at midday'. Ride the crest of the wave.

Receptive white

You may have chosen for your receptive white crystal a delicate, translucent snow quartz, a moonstone or a white matt pebble; receptive white stones temper the solar energies with gentler but no less lovely lunar light – indeed on occasions it can offer a better alternative to brilliant sunshine, which may blind us to objects and people on the horizon. This is the translucent light of the Moon that reveals spiritual potential, hidden forms and forces within us and the natural world. In our imaginations the Moon transforms trees into animals, and shadows into temples or shrines when bathed in moonlight – and so we can understand possibilities otherwise masked by daylight and reason.

Receptive white crystals are ruled by the lunar goddesses Diana (or Selene) of the classics and the ancient Egyptian Isis; the Moon has traditionally been regarded as the consort of the Sun, her silver to his gold, Queen Luna to King Sol in alchemy, and so these stones represent the anima: deep, unconscious, intuitive gifts and wisdom from ages past. The new beginning may be an inner one, perhaps the unfolding of psychic or divinatory abilities or a gradual move from material success to spiritual fulfilment.

If you cast a receptive white stone in a reading, this may indicate a slower, more gradual beginning, taking the first steps on a path that may not bear fruit for months or even longer. It may be that you cannot have your new beginning without hurting others who depend on you, or turning your back on commitments. And for every woman who makes a sudden break and walks away without suffering guilt or regrets, there are a hundred more who are aware of the interconnectedness of life, that what they say or do affects those around like a stone thrown in a pond – if a butterfly's wing motion can change the resonance of the universe, we sometimes have to tread softly on the path to personal fulfilment.

Reading two white stones
If you cast both a creative and a receptive white stone in a reading, at its best this promises the integration of animus and anima, so that after your momentous decision, you begin to make your dream come true, step by step. Let's take a mundane but common example: you begin a fitness regime because you want to be healthier. After the euphoric first day of low-fat eating and half an hour on your exercise cycle come the days when you have to work through your lunch hour and would usually rely on chocolate bars to see you through the deadline; or when you have been awake all night with a teething infant and only have moments to snatch a coffee and cake instead of breakfast.

Women especially find that the demands of the world tend to overtake their good intentions. So it is important to recognise that every change, whether it is taking a degree after retirement, working on meditation techniques, moving halfway across the globe to a new career or simply making time for yourself in a frantic schedule, involves a series of new beginnings each time you encounter an obstacle. So the two white stones promise real success if you persevere and accept that sometimes you will take a step or three backwards.

Choosing a crystal of the day

Each morning, you should select from your bag of crystals one that feels right, using your power hand – the one you write with. Take your time and let your fingers touch each stone in turn without trying to identify any of them. Draw one out and, cupping it between your hands, with your eyes closed, let any images that may act as a guide form in your mind. Once you know the meanings of each crystal you can apply these, but your impressions will always be the best guide and so you can select crystals without having learned the meanings.

Keep a crystal journal, which can be a fine vellum-bound book or a loose-leaf folder in which you can note your daily crystal. This will be most useful as you can look back at your record to see whether a pattern emerges. For example, your unconscious wisdom may prompt your hand to select white crystals five days in a row if you are hesitating about accepting an opportunity. You can also note down your crystal readings for yourself and others, and since the predicted events may take weeks or even months to become manifest in the material world, it can be helpful to record what was said, especially if a positive outcome seemed unlikely at the time of the reading.

The crystal you select each morning will contain the particular strengths you need for the day ahead. Carry your chosen crystal either wrapped in white silk or in a tiny drawstring bag and handle it frequently to absorb its special qualities, especially if the day is a difficult one.

If you feel yourself becoming dispirited during the day at home or work, wash your crystal of the day under a tap to remove physical impurities picked up in transit, soak it in a glass of mineral water for a few hours and then drink the water to absorb its energies by the old magical principle of physically taking in the magic. Alternatively, set the crystal on your work space to absorb the light, and see its coloured rays forming a circle of power and protection around you.

DAY 5
Black crystals

Black is the ultimate receptive colour and absorbs or negates all other colours. Hold your two black stones, your receptive black stone in your left hand and your creative black stone in your right, allowing the nurturing, calming yin energies to slow down your racing thoughts and fill you with the power not for *achieving* but of just *being*. Black crystals are ruled by Saturn or Saturnus, the Roman form of Cronus, god of time, who was deposed by his son Jupiter, after Cronus had refused to allow natural change and progression. But even this led to joy, because Saturnus was sent to Italy where he taught the farmers agriculture and engineering and established a golden age of peace and plenty.

At its most positive, black represents the ability to be open to others and to the world around us. These are the stones of waiting rather than rushing blindly into action and, most importantly, of natural endings, which, as happened with Cronus, lead to a deeper kind of happiness.

Reading black crystals

You will eventually need two different kinds of black stone but if you are starting with one, the key stone is the receptive one.

Creative black

You may have chosen a brilliant silvery black hematite, gleaming jet or jasper. All these stones have a rich sheen or deep blackness and are very different from the more muted hues of the receptive black stones; they are clear midnight as opposed to a misty dawn.

The idea of creative black may sound like a contradiction, but, as I said earlier, it is rarely all or nothing with crystals – or people. Creative black stones do hold a lot of energy, but the colour may indicate that you are wasting a lot of vital personal power either by holding on to a situation or relationship that is redundant or by suppressing negative and probably very justifiable feelings.

Creative black is the shadow side we all have, the angers and resentments that do so often give us the impetus for change. Once worked through, they allow all that lovely white potential to be released.

In divination, creative black stones represent a natural ending to a phase of life, whether it be the end of a time of living alone or the end of a relationship. Child-rearing involves many endings, not least the end of putting our own needs first. When children first go to school, then enter adolescence and eventually leave the nest, women lose a role that has centred around mothering for so many years that it has become a habit, sometimes long after it is needed.

Equally, a decision to be childless or celibate, or having these decisions imposed upon us, closes certain doors. Or we may be retiring from a chosen career or facing redundancy and trying desperately to hold on to what is familiar. Marriages and long-standing relationships may also need an occasional change of gear if they are to evolve and not stagnate, but that may involve dramatic reassessment of yourself as well as of your partner. People, especially men, who walk away from a long-standing relationship, are sometimes trying in vain to walk away from themselves.

Women also empathise with the endings in the lives of their partners, whether through illness, redundancy or retirement, and these may involve radical change in their own lifestyles. Such endings can be painful but there can be no new beginnings without them and it is only by embracing these change points, however they are caused, that we can move on to a whole new world of opportunities.

So whatever your personal ending, whether it is that career across the world I spoke of in the creative white crystals or your first months at college a thousand miles from home, or whether you are the one waving someone goodbye, temporarily or permanently, there is always sorrow involved in change and choice. Deep down women have *always* known that they cannot have pure undiluted happiness and that if you take one road there is another you cannot travel.

Receptive black

You may have found yourself a matt black pebble, perhaps a very dark piece of granite or flint, or bought some very dark grey or black smoky quartz or banded agate. Apaches' tears encapsulate all that is best about receptive black crystals with their promise that those who hold them will never know deep sorrow. That is not to say there will be no more sorrow in your life. But, however young they may be, women do share the sorrows of others and so in a sense draw strength from their empathy and ability to bring comfort. This ability begins in childhood with the first mewing kitten we cradle in our arms, or wild bird we rescue, and evolves to the moment we walk the final part of the road with a beloved dying relative or friend to whom we need to say goodbye.

Black receptive stones also talk of a deep well of acceptance of human frailty in yourself and others and the ability to see good in situations and people, however difficult. They are the crystals of the reality principle, the acceptance that compromise may be necessary and that being assertive and ambitious is very different from being ruthless.

You still have the desire to stop and take care of an injured animal or a depressed lover or friend even if you are late for an appointment, and it is that humanity that is your greatest strength – as long as you do not sacrifice your own needs to those of others so that you become resentful and trapped in a cycle of caring for everyone except yourself.

Reading two black stones

Having both black stones in a reading indicates that the issue involves your shadow side. Perhaps you feel you have no right to express anger or sorrow or to move on to the next stage in your life. Maybe you are fixed, through kindness rather than weakness or personal need, in the mothering role to your oversized baby birds – statistics show that many over-25s are either still living at home and paying far less than they would for accommodation elsewhere or have returned to the nest after a broken relationship; they are enjoying freedom and a good standard of living, while their parents may feel that they are lodgers in their own home. (I have partially solved this problem by buying myself a caravan to which I retreat periodically.)

Perhaps, as the only female in your workplace who is not on maternity leave or pregnant, you are doing double the work while others get tea and sympathy on tap. Whatever burden you are carrying for others, now is the time to lay it down. Use the creativity aspect of black to say 'No', whether to lazy employees, reluctant colleagues, ungrateful relatives or friends who assume that you do have time for them, day and night, whenever they feel like calling upon your agony aunt services. Every woman working from home will understand the dilemma. Now is the time to draw limits and start saying 'No'.

Red crystals

Hold your creative red stone in your right hand and your receptive red stone in the left and you will find it hard to stand still. For these are the crystals of movement and action, strength and courage. They are exciting but challenging, ruled by Mars, god of war (Ares in the Greek tradition). Mars was legendary father of Romulus and Remus, the founders of Rome. As god of both agriculture and war, he represented the ideal Roman, a farmer and a conqueror. But though fierce in battle, Mars possessed nobility of spirit and so these are the crystals of speaking or acting against injustice and inertia, the crystals of the crusader.

Reading red crystals

If you are only using one red crystal, make it the creative one.

Creative red

Whether you choose a garnet, a red agate or jasper or another vibrant red stone, the blood is coursing through your veins. Assertiveness in women is a trait that worries some men, who regard it as aggression; but sometimes it can be important to fight your corner – the Celtic queen Boudicca is still recalled for her courage against the Roman invaders of Britain and none, least of all her adversaries, dared brand her unfeminine.

The glass ceiling still exists in some areas of business and industry and a woman who has graduated from college or finished her training course with first-class qualifications may suddenly find that an older male executive expects her to make coffee and do his shopping simply because she is a woman. Or she may feel excluded when guys go to the pub or wine bar at lunchtime for what is still a male bonding ritual.

Promotion too can go to a man simply because it is still believed that 'women have babies and men have to support them'. Of course there are laws to stop the words being expressed openly, but there are a thousand and one ways of making life so difficult for a woman at work that she chooses to leave. For every spectacular tribunal case in which a woman is rewarded compensation for discrimination in the workplace, there are dozens of women with heavy financial or family responsibilities who suffer in silence because they cannot afford to speak out and risk losing everything.

Equality has come on in leaps and bounds since I first wrote on this topic. But some women in the armed forces and the police still experience sexism on a massive scale from colleagues. Even some apparently liberated husbands or partners can feel threatened if a woman's salary rises way above theirs. So because she loves him, or for the sake of family harmony, a woman lives with snide remarks about poor housekeeping or bad mothering, gets up earlier and cuts back on her own leisure time to prove that she can still care for the home and learns to praise his successes and diminish her own. In ten years' time, the thoughts in this section may have become outdated – but I fear not.

So it may be that you have to prove yourself every day in every way. But the creative red crystal offers you the power not only to survive, but to thrive. Creative red whispers to your inner ear that you know in your heart that it is time to strike out for what you really want to achieve, perhaps crusading on behalf of others. Perhaps you are already moving towards this achievement: you have great reserves of power if you focus single-mindedly on your personal goal. What is more, you are increasingly aware that acknowledging your own successes and strengths is not, as grandmother scolded, 'showing off', but recognising what you are and how far you have come (more of this in the section on orange crystals on pages 60–63).

Receptive red

You may have chosen a calcite, a fluorite, a banded agate, another of those Earth rainbows that hold gentle but enduring power, as your receptive stone. But if you enjoy searching around for your stones, look for a muted red pebble, usually sandstone or shale on hills or beaches, sometimes even in parks.

The power of receptive red crystals lies in perseverance and persistence in adversity or in situations where a goal seems to be taking far longer than anticipated. Think of soldiers marching mile after mile with heavy packs, of pioneers in their wagon trains with not much but hope, of seekers after the Holy Grail or pilgrims crossing mountain ranges to sacred shrines. All were driven by the need to reach a destination or to attain spiritual fulfilment. So if you feel that each time you make progress the goal seems to move further away, break down the way forward into a series of smaller steps and redefine your overall aim each time you attain one of the interim successes.

Receptive red, however, sometimes suggests that you are perhaps turning frustrations inwards, blocking your innate energy resources. So it is important to channel your energies – rather like a long-distance runner – and not waste power by becoming annoyed by the incompetence or unhelpfulness of others. Instead, learn to complain about that inefficiency or lack of input in a controlled but assertive way. 'I do mind', practised as a mantra ten times a day, is the best antidote to stress headaches; it also avoids projecting the full force of your accumulated anger on to a chocolate bar or an innocent supermarket cashier or railway official guilty of minor incompetence, rather than on to the true perpetrator at the end of a long frustrating day.

Reading two red stones
The two stones together generate what is sometimes called the *red raw kundalini*. This is root energy associated with Shakti, the Hindu Mother Goddess who danced on the inert body of her husband Shiva to restore him to life. So power is the predominant issue when both red crystals appear. It is an area of passion and sexuality, the instinctive energy that drives us ever forward to achieve, to initiate change, to travel, to fight for what really matters. Even normally docile animals will fight to the death to protect their young.

Power is still a difficult area for some women, especially older ones who were, like me, brought up to try always to smile, to cry only if things got bad and to defer to authority – especially male authority. Meanwhile, the boys were allowed to fight and shout if things went wrong. The majority of domestic violence still centres on bullying by husbands and fathers, but although I was very impressed when my older daughter broke her ex-boyfriend's nose when he hit her, I am not advocating physical violence. Rather, women should stake their claim to their own mental and emotional power and, having fought for equality, should not revert to playing the helpless female when the going gets tough.

Though women of some faiths are now admitted to the priesthood, the ultimate source of power, women priests to whom I have spoken in the UK still have problems with prejudice, from older women as well as men, and say that parishioners expect them to act as a mother to the flock.

Anger and aggression are still emotive issues – though well directed anger can be a powerful impetus for change and survival. So the combination of red crystals heralds exciting change, perhaps long-distance travel, or radical domestic or career moves, but above all an awareness of female power and potential.

As you continue to select your daily crystal, you may see patterns emerging that indicate hidden strengths or unacknowledged issues that should be resolved. You may find that drawing or painting a picture of your crystal impressions or putting them into verse or a story clarifies the issue – even if you pick exactly the same crystal each day, the images it evokes will change, as the area of experience unfolds.

Psychic protection

Once you begin crystal divination, you will be open to all kinds of psychic energies as your own psyche unfolds. The majority of these will be entirely benign.

Psychic protection is rather like ensuring that you give your e-mail address or phone number only to those whom you wish to contact you, rather than placing your name in a public directory. If you carry out crystal divination or rituals only when you feel positive and try to see the best in any situation or person, you have inbuilt protection, for everything is said to return threefold to the sender. But if you read crystals for others or are surrounded, as we all are at one time or another, by hostility or apathy, it can be helpful to protect yourself as you work, from your own buried negativity as well as that of others. The following are methods that I, or others with whom I have worked, find effective, but you can devise your own.

A circle of candles

✦ Surround yourself with a ring of small golden candles, if possible round ones, the shape of the Sun. Buy a store of these at Christmas when they are cheap and plentiful. Arrange them so that you can move safely within the ring without burning yourself.

✦ Begin in the south, the direction of the noonday Sun and light your candles in turn clockwise, saying:

Burn bright, candlelight, drive away all danger,

Protect me as I work and live, from false friend and stranger.

✦ Repeat this as a mantra until you see yourself surrounded by the light.

✣ Now turn nine times clockwise within the circle of candles and your pool of light, repeating the mantra.

✣ Sit within the circle of light and see it hardening like a transparent golden crystal shield above your head, beneath your feet and all around in a sphere.

✣ Blow out your candles anti-clockwise, beginning with the one immediately to the right of your southernmost candle so that the last candle alight is the first one you ignited.

✣ Watch the afterglow gradually fade, knowing that it is constantly present, although unseen by the physical eye.

✣ Repeat your candle ritual regularly whenever you feel the protection getting weaker. You can use this protective device, or any of the others I suggest or you devise, whenever you feel under threat or anxious.

Because it might not be practical to light a circle of candles every time you use your crystals, you can create a psychic short-cut to protection.

✣ Extend your hands so you can feel the edges of your psychic shield and see the circle of light beyond.

✣ Decide on your automatic protective activation mechanism. One method is to touch your unseen psychic Third Eye on your brow in the position between and just above your physical eyes and say:

> *Whenever I thus awaken my Third Eye,*
>
> *I will bring to life my candle circle of protection.*

Guardian angels

These benevolent spirits offer the most traditional form of psychic protection and can provide a specific focus for benign forces of light and love. Some people invoke angels to stand in each corner of the room, or a single guardian. These can be visualised as 'traditional' angels with golden wings or personal guides you may have encountered in dreams and past-life work – a sage, a nun or an ancient Egyptian priest, a priestess from Atlantis or a deceased kindly grandmother who, you sense, watches over you.

We all visualise and experience protection in our own way and your own guardian, however homely, is more effective than a formal invocation of the most glorious archangel to whom you may not relate in a personal sense.

When you have finished your psychic work, silently thank your protector(s) and because you have taken protection from the cosmos, restore balance by a small positive act towards someone in need of care – put out food for the birds, scatter a few seeds on a bare piece of land, or make a friendly phone call or write an encouraging letter to a person who has been unpleasant to you through personal unhappiness.

Protective crystals

Certain crystals have natural protective powers that you may use. Choose four small crystals from the ones listed and position them either in the corners of the room or on the four corners of the table where you are working. If you decide to adopt this form of protection, keep your protective crystals separate from your divinatory ones and wrap them in dark silk when not in use. Again they can be brought out whenever you feel vulnerable or if potentially confrontational people are visiting your home or workplace. Protective crystals traditionally include: black agate, amethyst, bloodstone, carnelian, garnet, black and red jasper, jet, lapis lazuli, obsidian, rose quartz, smoky quartz, sodalite, tiger's eye, topaz and turquoise.

Protection may also be obtained by placing a clear quartz or amethyst pyramid in front of you during psychic work. Alternatively, you may use a protective crystal on a chain or cord around your neck, in a ring or on a bracelet to act as a shield against any harm. The circular shape offers additional security. You can also carry a defensive crystal in your bag or pocket.

DAY 8
Crystal readings

While you can carry out readings to resolve problems and to make decisions, sometimes you will want to identify aspects of your life that are moving to the fore in the immediate future; or perhaps you want to find strengths that you can tap to maximise any opportunities on the horizon. As well as casting crystals on a cloth, which I will describe later, you can draw out three crystals from your bag, as a focus for problem-solving, decision-making or a life update.

When you have learned all the crystal meanings, this is a method of reading for other people that you can use absolutely anywhere. I have given hundreds of impromptu readings with the bag of crystals that I carry almost everywhere – on planes, ferries and trains, in cafés and while waiting at radio or TV stations.

But by tuning into the psychic impressions emanating from each stone selected, you can produce accurate readings for yourself and others even in the early stages of your crystal work. This is a stage you should continue to incorporate into readings, even when you are experienced.

A reading with three stones

With your own or the readings of others, you can either focus on a specific question or area, or allow the crystals to guide you.

÷ First, the person who is the subject of the crystal reading should touch the crystals inside the bag and select three that feel right, one after the other. Place the crystals in a row from left to right on the table or floor.

÷ If the reading is for yourself, hold in turn each crystal that you have selected, in the order of choosing, in your cupped hands.

÷ Let images, feelings, even words or fragrances form for each crystal before moving on to the next. These will often be in symbolic form. If you see nothing, imagine you are recounting the story of each crystal. Visualise it in a natural setting and gradually expand your range of vision so that you can see the surrounding area – a method that invariably enables you to link the images with your life.

÷ Interpret the next two crystals in the same way. The best readings I have made have been on late-night phone-ins when I am tired after two or more hours of broadcasting and close my eyes and let the words flow. On occasions I have amazed myself.

÷ When reading for others, ask the subject to hold each crystal in turn and to share any impressions with you.

÷ Then hold the chosen crystal yourself, allowing your own images to form; these will reflect the psychic impressions made on the crystal by the subject as he or she held it.

÷ When you have read all three crystals, you will find that they form a coherent picture that may link directly with the original question or offer an overview and suggest future paths.

When interpreting the crystals for others, remember that this is a psychic dialogue and that however pressurised you may be by the questioner, you must not suggest any particular course of action – he or she alone must make the decisions.

In the same way, if someone is unhappy or worried, it is tempting to promise them happier times around the corner. But it is more helpful to use the crystals to suggest positive steps that can be made towards reclaiming happiness or in making the most of any opportunities. If you sense troubles ahead, concentrate on future strategies to avoid any potential difficulties, and couch any warnings in terms of turning possible obstacles into advantages.

A crystal reading for Rachel

Rachel is a senior doctor in neurology in her early sixties living in the north of England; she has become increasingly interested in alternative healing techniques. She would like, on her impending retirement, to use her extensive medical knowledge to write a book combining the two strands of healing. However, she has encountered a great deal of hostility among her hospital colleagues about the 'weird ideas' that she has, in spite of their opposition, attempted to introduce into the area of post-operative care – with some success.

The head of Rachel's department says that if she writes a book linking conventional practice with spiritual healing and herbalism, she would cast doubt on the credibility of the medical textbooks she has already produced – and by implication on her department. Rachel finds herself on the horns of an apparently insoluble dilemma: should she go ahead with her book or retain the approval of her colleagues by taking yet another commission on methods that she no longer feels hold all the answers?

Rachel selects:

1 A creative red jasper.

2 A creative white crystal quartz.

3 A creative silvery black hematite.

All three crystals that Rachel has chosen are creative, which suggests that the answer lies in action and inspiration, rather than following the status quo.

Creative red

Rachel felt great heat coming from the red jasper and saw images of tall warrior women with exotically painted faces, striding through a tropical rainforest. They stopped at a clearing and placed fruit and flowers at the huge image of a goddess carved in red jasper. They knew that they might die because invaders were coming, but vowed that they would never betray their goddess by cowardice.

Red jasper is a stone of defence against hostility, offering stability and courage under difficulty. Rachel said that the hospital administrators had in their gift various lucrative lecturing positions that were usually offered to retired senior physicians and surgeons. But she has been told unofficially that if she continued with her alternative healing practices, she would be deemed unsuitable.

Creative white

The pure quartz, essence of the dragon, as it is known in the Orient, the *visible nothingness* of the Buddhists, seemed to Rachel to be surrounding her in pure white light that filled her with total certainty that her path was the right one. As the crystal of the Life Force, it suggested that retirement for Rachel could be the beginning of new kind of life, in which her spirituality would evolve.

Rachel says that her own spiritual healing powers have been evolving and she has noticed that she is able to alleviate post-operative pain by touch. She has started to explore crystal healing and is increasingly convinced that it is possible to enable patients to recover faster from operations by a combination of herbal baths and infusions and crystals.

Creative black

Even Rachel's black stone was creative, and as she held it she saw a clear sky filled with silver UFOs and a group of scientists on the ground shaking their heads and denying the evidence of their own eyes. Hematite is a protective stone, one that clears indecision, aids concentration, improves memory and helps all forms of study; it builds confidence, will-power and self-esteem, strengthens courage and acts as a shield against physical and emotional hostility. It also aids astral projection.

Rachel is aware that she would be closing the door on a potentially profitable way of life in financial terms, by going against official policy. But she is convinced that if she is meticulous in her research and writing she could encourage other open-minded doctors, some of whom are already using alternative practices – and perhaps even make sceptics reconsider the evidence.

The chosen crystals confirmed for Rachel the importance of listening to her inner wisdom and following the path that was right for her, regardless of the approval or disapproval of others.

Orange crystals

If you hold your creative orange crystal in your right hand and your receptive orange in your left, you will experience a sense of balance and harmony, of sun filtering through rich orange groves. For these are Sun crystals, but this is the Sun when it rises or sets and not the brilliant light of the white crystals.

Reading orange crystals

Amber is said to contain the power of many suns, and creative warmth radiates from this and other similar orange stones, melting rigid attitudes and assimilating what is of worth from any experience. These crystals of integration are associated with self-esteem and joy in our unique nature and give us the confidence to be the person we essentially are, without the need to adopt roles or follow stereotyped images created by the media. If you are only buying one orange stone, choose the creative orange as this is the key crystal for this colour.

Creative orange

You may have chosen amber, which is my own favourite because its antiquity emphasises the essential self which is always with us. Or you might have selected a carnelian, a jasper or another vibrant orange crystal. Creative orange crystals are concerned with originality. So perhaps you are becoming aware that your ideas and aims are different from those around you; you come up with inspirational solutions, begin a new project that is all yours, or you are planning a step towards independence or considering becoming self-employed, becoming a healer or studying advanced mathematics for fun. Perhaps you may be contemplating moving away from a familiar town, quitting the nest for the first time or a second time, after a false start – or maybe you are at a later stage, leaving behind adult children and grandchildren to run a bar in Spain or write a novel. The menopause, with or without HRT, marks for many women a chance to begin to live life on their own terms, aware that you cannot please everyone and be true to yourself.

At 50, after two husbands, five children and two very different careers, I am just beginning to unearth the real person behind Mrs Desperate-to-please and discovering (or rediscovering) my true, rather solitary nature, which I tried to overwrite in my efforts to adopt a persona that was a mixture between a Shakespearean tragic heroine and the whiter-than-white mother in the soap powder adverts.

What may seem a sudden impulsive decision may in fact be a step towards rediscovering the real you who was persuaded by the demands of the world to follow paths that, however, successful, left part of your essential nature unfulfilled. This is the positive aspect of those endings that were expressed in the black crystals and assures you of happiness and fulfilment if you follow your unique dreams.

Receptive orange

Whether you choose banded agate, calcite or beryl in a delicate, almost cloudy orange, or have found matt orange stones on a beach or hillside, your receptive orange crystal is like the sunlight behind clouds, or hidden on a misty morning, waiting for an opportunity to break through – present, but not visible.

Receptive orange stones may appear when we feel that our identity has been eroded. This often happens when women become mothers, but it can occur in any situation: a young woman who is in an unfulfilling job, tied by the need to earn money, perhaps in an area of high unemployment; an older woman seeing her new-found freedom disappearing as she is expected to care for a frail parent or her grandchildren; or any woman trapped in a marriage where love is buried beneath routine. Especially in these busy times when leisure can be taken up with chores or overtime, there may be moments for all of us when we cry: 'Where am I? Who am I? Do I exist any more?' and spiritual enhancement seems the province of wealthy women whose only task is to hone their already perfect bodies, minds and spirits.

But if you can begin even in small ways to make time, however short, for yourself, then gradually the unique person that is you will emerge. Begin to exercise your preferences – you may not even remember what they are. Turn round the questions 'Where am I?', 'Who am I?', 'Do I exist?' into an affirmation of power, spoken as you claim back those precious moments, from chores that others could take on, responsibilities that are not rightfully yours, but which you originally accepted with the best motives (more of this in the green crystals):

I am here and now, I am uniquely myself, I exist and am of worth,

as I am and who I am.

As you unfold the meanings of the crystals, you will find strong echoes between stones, especially those that are close to each other on the colour spectrum, for all the aspects of ourselves are interrelated and changes in one affect the others, for good or ill. In readings you may find that two crystals cast close together on the circle cloth (see Day 10 on pages 64–9) contain the same message in subtly different forms.

Reading two orange stones
If you select both orange stones, you are examining your boundaries, where you end and others begin. This is an issue that has troubled mystics and psychologists alike. We begin as part of our mother or, as some philosophers declare, as spirits in a world of bliss before birth to which we return after death. In pregnancy, women share their bodies again and a telepathic as well as emotional connection between mother and child seems to remain throughout life, although in extreme cases this can be destructive.

When people fall in love, we talk of two souls becoming one and some believe that we each have a twin soul, an alter ego that will make us complete. Some couples who spend a lifetime together may find it hard to be separate and one partner may not survive long after the death of the other. Some psychologists believe that teenage rebellion is a way of enabling the child to loosen the cords of connection especially with the mother and flee the nest. The psychologist Fromm speaks of the human fear that we are all ultimately alone.

So the orange stones together point to an issue to do with your perception of yourself, not necessarily a crisis of identity, but perhaps a milestone in a relationship that needs a change in the level or nature of commitment. Do you *want* a deeper level of commitment in a relationship? Does the other person? Do you want to start a family or are you happier as a twosome or alone? Is this a time to concentrate on your career, and, if so, is promotion and becoming more involved in your current place of employment important to you? Do you want to move on or to strike out alone? Is your priority to evolve spiritually, to develop your psychic awareness? Others can off-load their expectations, like the parents who want to see a daughter settled, or wish to become grandparents, who cannot understand why she needs to end a relationship. Why give up a successful career in the media to open an animal sanctuary or make beautiful but non-commercial ceramics? A partner may resent your need to go off alone for a week to visit Celtic churches, or just sit in the sunshine and watch the butterflies.

The key to the double orange stones lies in deciding what you and you alone want, both immediately and in the future. This may not be an all-or-nothing decision; you may be able to go off alone for a while but remain in a close relationship, or perhaps you can keep your job but refuse promotion to allow time for other aspects of life to merge. It really is a question of deciding your own priorities and – most importantly – setting your own parameters.

DAY 10

Casting the stones

✛

The most powerful crystal divination occurs when the stones are cast on to a cloth. This is a traditional method, adapted for modern practice, that I also use with my runes, for it is one that permeated the ancient world as a way of interpreting stones of all kinds. Each area of the casting cloth represents a different level of experience; by interpreting crystals that fall in each realm, you can understand more clearly the relationships between the stones, and pinpoint specific areas of your life where positive energy or input is needed.

Sit in a pool of sunlight as you work or use pure white candles at the four main compass positions. You will need a piece of fabric about 50 centimetres (20 inches) square in a dark colour so you can see the crystals against it. A plain square scarf is ideal.

Draw three concentric circles in the centre of the cloth. I draw my circles and markings in gold permanent marker pen, but you can use plain black or any colour that shows clearly.

The easiest way is to draw around three inverted plates in size order, the smallest first, the size of a saucer for the innermost circle, followed by a tea plate and finally a dinner plate. Alternatively you can use three inverted bowls of different sizes – pasta sets are ideal.

Some people use a pair of compasses, but as long as you have an area of unmarked cloth about 10 centimetres (4 inches) around the outside of the largest circle, you need not be exact. The first circle should have a radius of about 6.5 centimetres (2½ inches), the second about 12.5 centimetres (5 inches) and the third about 19 centimetres (7½ inches).

Experiment on paper until you produce the right result and cast crystals on to it to see whether the dimensions work in practice.

You may wish to create one cloth for your own work and a second for reading for others. You may like to sew running stitches around each circle, as you do so visualising light entering each stitch and filling the cloth with positive energies. Your cloth, when it is finished, will look something like this:

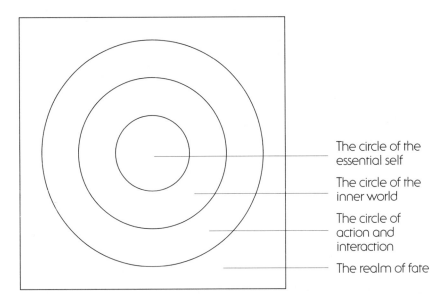

The circle of the essential self

The circle of the inner world

The circle of action and interaction

The realm of fate

The circle of the essential self

The innermost circle talks of the core issues in life, fundamental beliefs, the essential person you were as a small child before the world intruded, who remains basically unchanged throughout all the stages of womanhood. So this circle marks the boundaries of this essential you – as opposed to the you who has a lover, family, friends or colleagues – the person that is you after everyone else has gone away or is asleep; the you who sits alone, but not lonely, complete and separate, a unique body, mind and soul.

Crystals that fall in this area are of great significance in both the immediate and long-term future, and usually suggest independent action or an original solution.

Here too lies your untapped potential, your personal evolutionary blueprint for worldly, mental and spiritual development, which unfolds gradually through your life and may be modified by circumstances or other people, but which always bears your personal hallmark.

Through developing these potential destinies, rather than following blind fate or other people, you will automatically attain ever higher levels of awareness, so that you experience deeper pleasure and insight even in quite mundane moments, and start to understand the patterns of existence and your own unique place in this interconnected universe.

This is an important circle and if it is frequently empty, you may be giving too much to others and your life may be filled with too many disparate elements. You may need time to *be* rather than to *do* and the space to reconnect with your centre.

The circle of the inner world

The middle circle is the circle of your inner world of thoughts and emotions, where conscious and unconscious worlds meet, where reason and intuition can work in harmony, bringing together the left and right sides of the brain into an integrated whole.

Crystals that fall here indicate that it is a time to formulate plans and listen to dreams that may hold solutions and initiate new paths of life. Sometimes unexpected crystals can be cast here, for example a clear creative white crystal when you had considered your life settled and untroubled. Our minds are never still and your psychic antennae may already be tuning into future opportunities or deep-seated desires that may be felt, not immediately, but in weeks or even months.

This is the area least troubled by constraints of space and time, where you can rehearse endings and beginnings, achieve successes, win battles and master unfamiliar processes. What is more, by the mysterious and largely untapped powers of the mind and psyche, using the powers of visualisation (focused imagination) and empowerments or mantras (concentrated declarations of intent), you can transfer power to bring about the manifestation of your plans and desires in the outer world, to turn your dreams into reality.

Our inner voice can be our most accurate guide to action if we listen to it and filter out those superfluous but strident voices giving conflicting advice both within our heads and via the opinions of those around us. It can warn us of potential hazards, untrustworthy people or situations that may on the surface appear reliable but turn out to be false. Conversely, this inner voice may offer reassurance if the future seems uncertain.

Crystals in this circle can reinforce the rightness of decisions we were contemplating and help us to separate our innate wisdom from the free-floating anxieties that dull imagination and block rational planning.

The circle of action and interaction

The outer circle is the area of action and relationships, not only with lovers and partners, but with family, friends, colleagues and officialdom.

Crystals that fall here indicate interaction with others, communication, negotiation, whether to persuade others to your point of view or to adapt your plans or actions, without losing sight of the inner person of the first circle or the dreams of the second. It is the realm of putting your thoughts and plans into action and of making tangible progress towards achieving material success or personal happiness, or resolving problems.

So whether you are initiating a new venture or stage of your life, declaring love or saying goodbye, sending your book to a publisher, planning a holiday or spring-cleaning your life, whether you are 18 or 80, the open road of life is calling. You should seize any opportunities for new experiences, for meeting new people, trying new activities, and aim high, especially if you have a number of creative crystals in this circle.

If there are mainly receptive crystals in your circle of action, the spring-cleaning aspect should come to the fore and you may need to shed burdens that you need no longer carry, but continue to do so out of habit. Consider what changes would bring happiness to you – as opposed to those people around you. Even though your options may be limited, maximise whatever opportunities you have and try to do something, however small, that will give you pleasure. Call in all those favours and offers of help and for once let tomorrow take care of itself.

The realm of Fate

The crystals that fall outside the three circles, but remain on the cloth in the outer segment, the realm of Fate, are of great significance. They represent what is soon to be moving into the subject's life, and crystals in this area, the realm of waiting, suggest that no action should be taken; allow events to unfold and wait for others to react or to make decisions that may affect your future plans. This can, in a sense, represent the most difficult area of all – you may have to accept that a long-awaited new beginning, whether it be a domestic or career move, must be delayed or that it is not the time to initiate change or to speak out. But it can equally be a very fruitful area, when you allow seeds to take root and events to take their course.

Modern society demands instant gratification: we are constantly in search of instant success, love, sex and happiness, to replace the redundant, outmoded, unlovely or outworn. But the older world talks of cycles and seasons and says that to each purpose there is a time and a season. So when crystals fall in this area, it is a time to wait, and grow stronger within.

On the runic cloth this area is called Is, meaning Ice, the fifth element in the Viking world where ice and snow would make travelling impossible and the people had to wait for the ice to melt, so becoming rested and stronger and ready for when spring came. Modern heating and lighting turn night into day, winter into summer, but our bodies and spirits suffer from the loss of the darker days when people would rest and sleep more – and, on a spiritual level, that is what this segment of the cloth is recommending.

When you cast your crystals, one or more may fall outside the three marked circles, on the area of the cloth that denotes the realm of fate – or what is yet to come – or even on the floor. Over the years I have modified the way I use the circle cloth. At one time I would interpret crystals that fell outside the circles even if they were on the floor or table. But I have obtained far more accurate readings since I have disregarded those that fall outside the cloth.

I now cast another crystal to replace any that fall off the cloth and in practice the new crystal may land anywhere and – like all unexpected factors – change the tenet of the reading. The more crystals needed to complete the three, six or nine cast, the more fluid the situation, and if you do have to use a large number you may benefit from a second cast a few days later to see what is moving into your life.

DAY 11
A cast of three

For this reading you will use all 20 stones. The ones whose meanings you have not learned, you can read intuitively. Let words and pictures form as you hold each in your cupped hands.

✣ Ask a question or focus on an area of your life that is predominant.

✣ Take time to run your fingers over the 20 crystals in the bag and draw out three that feel right, one at a time.

✣ Holding the crystals in your power hand (the one you write with), about 15 centimetres (6 inches) from the cloth, cast them either singly in the order you selected them or the three together.

✣ Aim for the centre of the cloth – this is where psychokinesis comes in: no matter how carefully you think you are aiming the crystals, they invariably either fall together in the relevant circle or scatter in different directions.

✣ If one or more is outside the cloth, place it on the table and select more crystals from the bag, so that three do fall on the cloth. If it takes several casts, there may be a great deal of indecision or conflicting choices around you.

✣ Consider the grouping of the crystals, whether they are far apart or clustered.

✣ Now interpret the stones separately, beginning with the first one cast if you threw them singly or in the order that seems the most significant. Alternatively, begin with the crystals in the innermost circle and work outwards.

✣ If you are reading for someone else, you can ask them which is the key stone. As with your crystal of the day, hold each crystal in your cupped hands before returning it to the appropriate circle. Ask the person for whom you are reading to hold each stone and give any impressions they may have before handing it to you.

✛ If you know the colour meaning, add this information, plus the receptive or creative significance.

✛ If two of the same colour are cast, then this issue is a key one.

✛ Finally, consider the reading as a whole. If this is difficult, tell a story based around the three stones and the significance will become clear in the symbols that your unconscious mind spontaneously suggests.

A crystal reading for Annie

In this book, I have tried to provide a representative sample of readings for women of all ages. The following is a dilemma that I have encountered many times among friends and colleagues over the past few years and have experienced myself. It is perhaps the one that is most devastating, especially where the woman has been with her partner for many years and genuinely had no inkling there was a problem. Of course women too can have extramarital relationships and sometimes leave partner and children behind for a new lover. But my research suggests it is more usually the woman who is betrayed, not only when she has put her own career on hold to care for children, but when she may have jumped through hoops to maintain a successful career and a happy relationship. Infidelity may occur at a time when a man begins to notice he is physically ageing, as a way of attempting to recapture his youth and virility.

If a man is quite a high earner or in a power position, he can seem attractive to a younger woman and yet vulnerable – and will treat his lover with a devotion never displayed towards his wife. We have all heard: 'My wife doesn't understand me', 'I stay only for the children' and 'We haven't had sex for years'.

Annie lives in Toronto. Her husband Greg left her and their school-age children 18 months ago to live with his personal assistant. She has re-established herself full-time in the teaching career that she had scaled down to care for the family, as Greg was away a great deal on business. She has recently started dating again; the children have seen their father only periodically, as his new partner does not like contact with his first family.

But suddenly the new relationship has broken up: Greg's new partner was pressing him to start a family which he did not want and Greg has asked Annie if he can move home. The children are eager to have their father back and Greg is vowing eternal love and devotion. But Annie has started to enjoy an independent life in spite of the difficulties and is very uncertain of her feelings towards Greg. She casts:

1 A creative black crystal: an agate in the circle of her inner world.

2 A creative orange crystal: a carnelian in the circle of the essential person.

3 A receptive white crystal: a moonstone in her outer area of Fate.

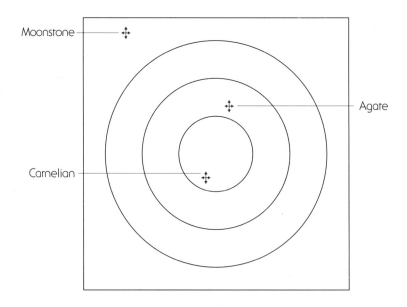

The **creative black crystal** in the circle of her inner world suggests that Annie still has a great deal of unresolved anger and resentment at Greg's betrayal; this has been brought to the surface by Greg's assumption that she has lived frozen in time and he can return as though nothing had happened. Some men are very good at emotional amnesia and Greg is an expert.

As Annie held the agate, she saw in her mind's eye huge black birds suddenly emerging from a cave and herself trying to drive them back, but being attacked in the process. She realised that whether or not Greg was to enter her life again, part of her had died and that she must mourn the loss of what had seemed a very happy marriage before moving on to what would be essentially a new relationship. Sometimes we can be so busy coping that our own emotional loss becomes buried.

The **creative orange crystal** in the circle of the essential self confirms the strength that Annie has acquired since Greg deserted her. As she held the carnelian, she saw a blood-red sun rising over sand, huge pyramids and herself walking alone across the desert, entirely at peace. Annie's sister had promised to care for the children while Annie went on holiday to Egypt, for Egyptian history was an interest Annie had developed since Greg's departure, and she was planning to take a part-time diploma in Egyptology. Annie has rediscovered her strong, separate identity that had become submerged in the demands of marriage and family and she is unwilling to lose this again.

The **white receptive crystal** outside the main circles represents the lunar wisdom that is as important as the more logical solar awareness. Any beginning would have to be slow, for Annie would need to learn to love, if not trust, Greg once more. Her feelings are paramount, far more important than what suits Greg – or even the children. Like many women in similar situations, Annie had shielded the children from knowledge of their father's desertion and made excuses when he could not see them.

As she held the moonstone, Annie saw a Crescent Moon and women robed in white, lighting torches to greet the Moon in a dark, woodland glade. Because the stone is in the area of Fate, this is not a time for action, but for waiting and letting events unfold. This is what her intuition, as represented by the moonstone, is telling her and it will take many months for Greg to establish a new relationship with her and the children, whether or nor they live together again. Her intuition also warns her that the speed with which Greg can abandon his new love and switch back to 'loving husband and father' mode indicates that he has learned little from his mistakes and basically wants a pressure-free existence.

Of course, Annie would not base so vital a decision on one reading, but it did confirm the rightness of her decision to proceed with caution – and not to give up her independence instantly.

DAY 12

Yellow crystals

If you hold your creative yellow crystal in your right hand and your receptive yellow in the left, indecision and confused thoughts will be replaced by clarity and focus, as though someone had opened a window in your mind and clear morning light came flooding through. For yellow is the colour of mind power, of logic, learning and communication – and illumination through deduction and a rapid assimilation of the facts. Yellow crystals are ruled by Mercury, the Roman winged messenger of the gods (known as Hermes to the Greeks).

Bearing a healing rod, called a caduceus, entwined with two serpents that could induce sleep, Mercury carried communication between the heavens, Earth and the underworld. Through his skill and dexterity, he came to rule over commerce and medicine and also became patron of tricksters and thieves. So your yellow stones have this quicksilver quality to help you write, speak, calculate the chances of success or extricate yourself from difficult situations. If you are buying only one crystal in this colour, choose creative yellow as this is the key stone.

Reading yellow crystals

Creative yellow

Whether you have selected a sparkling yellow citrine, a topaz, a zircon, a rich opaque yellow jasper or some other creative yellow stone, the way forward lies in using your head and not in relying on your heart or your intuition. Here it is the animus qualities that come to the fore, but your actions and responses will be swift and focused, not the measured considerations of the blue stones that are ruled by Jupiter.

There may have been confusion around you – perhaps someone is being less than open with you – but you have the ability to cut through indecision and to see your way clearly. Communication is also a key factor and you can ask for what you need and express your opinions, knowing that reason is on your side and that you can persuade others to your point of view with ingenious but realistic arguments.

It is a good crystal for computer work, for technology, for anything to do with the media and memory, for pushing through a business deal or for acquiring new skills. However, when this crystal appears, it is often your mind that gains fresh perspectives, and any travel will turn out to be work-related or a last-minute decision to take a short holiday. No shrinking violets here – you are making real inroads into whatever your current aim may be. Many a first book has been created under the auspices of this crystal, though novels are more under the rulership of the purple crystals. Beware irritability and change for change's sake

Receptive yellow

These stones include calcite, fluorite, rutilated quartz and soft, cloudy, golden beryl. The shore, hills and parks are a treasure trove of receptive, matt, yellow pebbles, of limestone, sandstone or shale. I have a very soft yellow quartz I found on my local beach on the Isle of Wight. It looks quite dull but when you hold it to the sunlight you can see the luminescence and it is excellent for gradually clearing indecision and restoring perspective during a dark night or week of the soul.

These represent the healing aspect of yellow, especially of your own inner doubts and confusion. You may be unsure in your own mind what it is you really want or perhaps you are overwhelmed by the seeming expertise of others. Equally, you may not be hearing what is actually being said and this can lead to unnecessary misunderstandings.

Sometimes, especially in painful situations or ones where we have experienced failure or rejection in the past, we put up barriers and admit defeat in advance by anticipating the condemnation or superior knowledge of others. These can be voices in your head of those who years earlier criticised you and foretold failure – parents, teachers, ex-lovers, former employers or colleagues – the effects of past spite or jealousy of others can hurt years after the event.

This is where the logic of yellow is so valuable in spring-cleaning the attics of our minds. Leave yesterday's rejections behind and negotiate each situation afresh. If you are currently the victim of gossip, jealousy or the malice of others, communicate your hurt or displeasure rather than absorbing it, in a clear but non-condemnatory way, and try to understand what it is that is causing the negative feedback.

Sometimes others can attack rather than face their own inadequacies, and this is where your healing powers can be at their most effective, turning enemies into friends by focusing on their problems.

Reading two yellow stones
The head rather than the heart is quite wrongly associated with purely male thinking and the success of many women especially in areas of communication is in the combination of the strength of the two aspects of the yellow crystals: the logic and single-mindedness of the animus, together with an awareness that issues are not always clear-cut and that the most straightforward solution is not necessarily the best. So, although the way may seem clear and your words, whether spoken or written, may seem unambiguous, you may be misunderstood. Everyone carries a personal agenda in their heads and two people can hold a conversation without listening to each other; many deteriorating relationships hit this problem.

There is something very important you need or want to communicate – the appearance of both yellow crystals confirms that. But the best computer program is only as good as its programmer and so you may need to go over the same ground many times, in a variety of ways, especially where there has been a history of difficulties – ingenuity may be the key to persuading others and seeing the situation from the other person's point of view in order to overcome any reservations. A lover or partner may perceive your suggestions about joint money management as an attempt to diminish his self-esteem, especially if you earn more than he does – the problem arises less in relationships between women. At work, if you are senior to traditionalist men, they may find it hard to accept even the most tactful criticism. In both cases, underlying insecurity may turn your words into a perceived attack. Or a female relative or friend may become emotional if you attempt to extricate yourself from a long-standing commitment, whether it is a weekly visit or a daily phone call that eats into your own time, or help you offered in a crisis that has become a habit. You may need to defuse the situation with the gentle humour and detachment of Mercury even though her sense of rejection is not justified – more of this in the green stones.

Green crystals

Hold your creative green crystal in your right hand and your receptive in the left and your heart will fill with love towards family and friends and compassion towards those who are ill or vulnerable; you may sense a connection with people and creatures, even plants and stones, which indigenous peoples such as the Native North Americans believed were infused with the same living spirit of divine creation.

For green crystals are stones of the heart and when we choose them in a reading it is our heart, not our head, that is speaking. They are ruled by Venus, whose Greek name was Aphrodite, 'born of the foam', beauty incarnate, the Roman goddess of love and seduction. So these are the stones of relationships, love, marriage and all affairs of the heart. Gentler romantic relationships and those involving friends, children, relatives and animals tend to be represented by the pink stones, which are also crystals of Venus. There is no clear demarcation line, except that the emotions ruled by green crystals tend to be more powerful ones.

They are also crystals of concern for the environment and a sense of responsibility for the fate of the rainforest, endangered species and the effects of pollution. More of this in the brown crystals, the other colour of Gaia or Mother Earth. If you are buying only one crystal in each colour, choose the receptive green.

Reading green crystals

Creative green

Through these vibrant green stones, aventurine, bloodstone, cat's eye, jasper and malachite, courses the Life Force. Hence creative green crystals – and receptive ones such as moss agate and jade –

are associated with growth of all kinds, and money-making in the sense of the gradual increase of wealth through endeavour, rather than the speculation indicated by the yellow crystals. For every aspect of green is directed towards a purpose that involves the well-being of others.

But creative green crystals primarily talk of following your heart, which may be in the Venusian sense of intense love or passion but is often much wider in its significance.

You may feel a desire to travel or move house, but unlike the action of the red stones, this is usually prompted by a particular location or incident in your life that has stirred yearnings deep within. Or you may meet someone new and know instantly he or she is the most important person in the world. We all have moments when life suddenly becomes vibrant, and energy, excitement and joy flow like the tide. Emotions are often described as flowing water and the ancient element of Water is in Jungian psychology associated with feelings. A door of opportunity opens and suddenly it seems as though there is no real alternative – and yet you may hesitate. This is very different from an impulse, because your heart is telling you that this is the right thing to do.

Following your heart may involve going off alone to save turtles, fight poverty or write a screenplay, declaring your love and risking rejection or the disapproval of others, giving up a career to stay at home with young children because you want to be the one to help their potential unfold, or caring for your sick mother because you want, rather than feel obliged, to return the care she gave you as a child. Perhaps your new suitcases are packed for college, but your heart says you should stay and marry the guy next door. Or the wedding may be booked and the dress hanging on the back of your door when you suddenly realise that you have a lot of growing up still to do and need to explore the urban jungle or go where the sunsets are beautiful and try to make it as an artist.

Such choices may not be mutually exclusive, but where there is disparity, you may have to hurt others a little and accept responsibility for causing pain, rather than making yourself and them unhappy in the long term. If we ignore these promptings from the heart, we may regret years later taking the safe course. T.S. Eliot in *The Four Quartets* refers to 'the door we did not open to the path we did not take ...'

Receptive green

These crystals include calcite, chrysoprase, jade and moss agate, whose green tendrils enclose a complex web of growth. It is no accident that these are stones of gentle healing, especially jade, for receptive green crystals symbolise empathy and sensitivity towards the feelings of others and especially those we love. When a receptive green crystal appears in a reading, it is a time to be aware of what lies beneath the surface. What people say can be very different from what they mean, and where there is a complexity of emotions involved, you need to listen rather than talk and to wait rather than act until true feelings do emerge, especially if a relationship has reached a transitional stage and you are uncertain of either your own feelings or those of the other person or people involved.

If you trust your feelings and listen to your heart, you *will* make the right choice. 'Going with the flow' was a phrase popular in the 1960s that reflects the older profound Chinese Taoist philosophy of allowing life to follow its natural course. If you are experiencing either great joy or sorrow, your receptive crystal says that it is important to let time and events restore the balance

Receptive green crystals also talk of relating to people as individuals with strengths and weaknesses, rather than in terms of the role which they adopt toward us. Most of us have encountered a possessive father or mother who cannot accept that a son or daughter is now an adult, perhaps with a family of their own. Conversely, it can be hard to shake off the expectations of society and realise that our children do not own us and that because we are a mother or grandmother, we do not have to be treated as an on-tap social worker and guardian angel.

At work, if a manager is acting apparently maliciously or autocratically it can help to visualise them as a small child who is unable to share their toys with others. I mentioned this in connection with the receptive yellow crystals. The office dragon may feel threatened by a younger woman and resent her apparent freedom. Or she may fear for her own position in an age where redundancy, especially of older people, is commonplace. A hostile mother-in-law may genuinely feel displaced in her son's affections, especially of she is alone or has an unhappy marriage. A possessive, critical grandmother can be trying to justify her own mothering practices or rewriting her experiences as a mother. Perhaps we idealise lovers or mentors in the workplace and are then disappointed when they turn out to have feet of clay. If we can understand the person behind the mask, not as an angel or demon but as a person with fears and needs like our own, then we can break a cycle of unsatisfactory interactions and replace them with positive ones.

Reading two green stones
If you get both green stones in a reading, emotions may be running high and you may be subject to emotional pressure to give way on an issue, perhaps concerning the change that would occur if you followed your heart.

Those closest to us may have a vested interest in our *not* changing. Older partners especially can worry if a woman suddenly wishes to expand her horizons. But even the New Man can turn into Old Father Traditionalist once his partner becomes a wife and/or mother, for the old patterns of his childhood may suddenly re-emerge. And nothing evokes more complex emotions in a man than his relationship with his mother.

Emotional leeches may not be malicious; they may simply be a possessive parent, an elderly relative who has alienated all his or her carers, an ex-boyfriend or -partner who refuses to let go or children who are all too quick to play the guilt game when left with a babysitter while a mother is working or, perish the thought, enjoying a few hours of leisure. There is also the adult infant who still relies on his or her mother to resolve every dilemma; the friend who telephones or arrives at the door each time a minor crisis occurs, and will not take a hint that this is not a good moment; colleagues at work who expect us to do more than our share because they have problems at home with love life or health, long after the original crisis has passed.

Women are naturally sympathetic to the needs of others and hate to see those around them in distress; this is our greatest strength and a source of positive creative energy. But emotional blackmail can, if not resisted, prevent us from being happy without feeling guilty. I have witnessed the most assertive executives trying to placate a troublesome relative on the phone before a crucial business meeting. Recently I witnessed Eleanor, a very experienced, professional television presenter, whose babysitter had let her down, bringing her toddler along to the live magazine show she fronted. The infant was clinging to her as she was due to go on to the set and refused to be placated by those around who offered to care for him during the show. Though Eleanor performed superbly as always, she was anxious the whole time she was on air. Her child, however, sensing when his co-operation was not crucial, had gone off to play happily before the show.

Women may be able to have it all, but until we can remove the guilt caused by those who would pull our heart strings, it is sometimes going to be an uphill struggle.

A circle reading with six stones

We have now covered the meanings of 12 stones, so you can try a divinatory reading by casting six stones, as two sets of three, on to the cloth. You can cast the stones separately in order of choosing if you prefer, but should select them in sets of three. The more stones you throw, the more significant the clustering of stones becomes. You can also, as with the cast of three, assess the relative mood of the reading according to whether more creative or receptive stones are cast or whether the reading has more balanced energies.

The fall of crystals in the different circles can indicate the overall emphasis of the reading, whether for example the question is a core one, concerned with individuality, which would be indicated by a predominance of crystals in the circle of the essential self. In contrast, an even distribution of crystals in the main circles suggests that the issue touches every aspect of life.

Once again you can use the intuitive impressions of the stones you do not know to supplement any crystals whose meanings you have not learned.

Caryn's reading

I met Caryn just before she left the UK to return to her native Australia. She was in her early twenties and had been working her way around the world for 18 months. Now she was undecided whether to go back to her mother's home in Adelaide where she had been offered a job with her uncle's accountancy firm to complete her charter, or to accept a job from some Australians she had met in Los Angeles, helping to produce and present a series of low-budget programmes about the old Aboriginal Trails. This would mean her living an essentially nomadic life for six months.

Caryn was passionate about Aboriginal customs and was eager to promote the most positive aspects of what she fears is a declining culture. At university, she had taken courses in media studies and worked on the university radio station as a presenter, though her main subject was mathematics.

If the Aboriginal project went well, there would be at least another year's work. But the money would be very poor and her widowed mother was eager for Caryn to return to a secure career. More crucially in her mother's eyes, Caryn could settle down with the boy next door, whom Caryn had dated since high school and who, her mother assured her, was waiting eagerly for her return.

Caryn cast:

1 **A citrine:** a creative yellow crystal in the circle of the essential self.

2 **A malachite:** a creative green crystal also in the circle of the essential self that almost covered the first crystal.

3 **A jade:** a receptive green stone in her circle of the inner world, in a position that was very close to the first two stones.

4 **A banded agate:** a receptive orange stone also in her circle of the inner world.

5 **A clear quartz:** a creative white crystal in the outer circle of action and interaction.

6 **A jet:** a creative black crystal also in her outer circle of action and interaction. This fell very close to the white crystal.

Caryn cast more creative than receptive crystals and so the overall mood of the reading is dynamic, suggesting action and change. She cast two crystals in each of the circles and the first three and last two formed clusters, demonstrating that these aspects were closely connected; the decision she had to make touched on every area of her life. There was nothing in the area of Fate, indicating that Caryn was in control of her life. However, this realisation was obscured by the influence of others on her decisions.

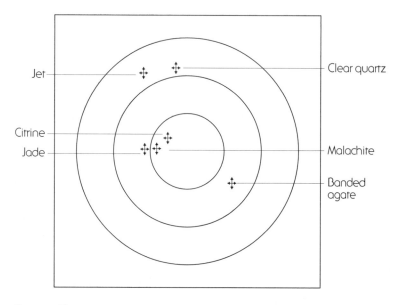

Creative yellow

This is the stone of communication, with links with the media. In the circle of the essential self, it indicates that Caryn's desires to make films about Aboriginal customs would offer her more fulfilment on a personal level than returning home to a job for which she admits she has little enthusiasm. But yellow is also the stone of logic, of using her head and of learning.

As she held the stone, she saw in her mind's eye a golden bird flying towards the sun. Caryn commented that she felt that she had discovered her potential for the first time in her travels, and did not want to be restricted by the old boundaries.

She did fear that perhaps she was being irresponsible in wanting to pursue an uncertain media career – a fact her mother stressed in her letters and phone calls. But Caryn said that if she returned to the world her mother had created for her, it would be due to emotional pressure, rather than free choice. Although Caryn had obtained a moderate degree in mathematics, she was not especially gifted in that field and it had been in media studies that she had shone. What is more, even if her new project was not a success, she would always have her mathematics qualifications to fall back on.

Creative green

This is the stone of following your heart and as Caryn had travelled and met new people, she had realised that in her life in Adelaide she had been fulfilling the dreams of her mother, who had given up her own maths degree course years before when she was pregnant with Caryn. Caryn's late father had been an accountant, as had his brother and father, so Caryn, the only child, had followed the family tradition. But her passion was the world of the indigenous peoples of Australia.

As she held the stone, Caryn saw rich, green, flowing waterfalls and fast rivers and herself negotiating the rapids, experiencing not fear but pure excitement. The fact that the green stone almost covered the yellow indicated that following her heart should predominate.

Receptive green

Two green crystals indicate that emotions are running high and there is emotional pressure on Caryn to return home. Her mother has made many impassioned phone calls and in her letters emphasised how lonely she is and how Caryn's former boyfriend Craig also is pining for her. Craig too has written letters assuming their relationship will continue as before and that they can get married on her return, although Caryn told him when she left Adelaide she was uncertain of her feelings.

Now, as she held her jade, she felt as though she was enclosed in a green silent pyramid, totally alone, totally at peace and complete in herself.

The pressure to conform has reached her thoughts and she admits that she feels guilty at letting Craig and her mother down, as well as her uncle who is eager for her to follow the family tradition.

Receptive orange

Caryn's identity has been much in her thoughts and as she has moved away from her family and home she has become aware for the first time that she does have very different aspirations from her mother and Craig. Significantly, she says that her boyfriend should have been her mother's son, as their world view is so similar. Craig is a trainee accountant with her uncle's firm.

Here she sees a setting sun, merging into darkness, and feels a sadness. She realises this is connected with the end of her trip that has in a sense postponed the need to answer the unresolved issues she left behind. She fears losing the confident, open person she has become if she goes home.

Creative white

A new beginning is indicated, seizing opportunities in the outer circle of interaction, and so Caryn realises that she cannot run away from the constricting past and the people who love her but unwittingly suffocate her individuality. The white crystal in her hand forms an image of a climber, trying to negotiate a snowy pass, but being constantly pulled back, and she notices that the safety rope is actually impeding his progress.

If she is to have a new beginning and be truly free, she needs to negotiate with her family and former boyfriend and go, if not with their blessing, at least not with them weighing on her mind. Above all, she has to let go of the security net she has clung to without realising it – that her home is waiting if things go wrong.

Creative black

The final stone, representing closing the door on what is redundant, is closely linked by its position on the cloth with the new beginning. She sees a huge black door in a dark tree and beyond it a dark passage leading to a point of light.

Caryn decides to go home and explain her plans, and the way that she has changed over the period she has been travelling, to Craig, her mother and uncle. She is also going to suggest that her mother completes the long-abandoned mathematics degree and so fulfils her own dreams. This way she will be truly mistress of her fate.

DAY 15
Blue crystals

As you hold a creative blue stone in your right hand and a receptive in the left, you are connected with the boundless energies of the Sky. For Jupiter, known as the 'Sky Father', the supreme Roman god, ruler of the universe, controls both blue and purple stones. Like his Greek counterpart Zeus, Jupiter controlled the thunderbolts, which were carried by his eagle, king and noblest of the birds. However, he ruled, not despotically, but as the chief of a triumvirate of gods, the other two being Juno, his consort, and Minerva, goddess of wisdom, who made up the feminine principle of deeper, more instinctive wisdom. Blue stones represent expansion in every way, wisdom, tradition, power, ambition, joy through fulfilment of objectives and justice. If you are buying only one stone of each colour, buy the creative blue.

Reading blue crystals

Creative blue

Whether you choose the power stone, turquoise, or its substitute sky-blue howzite, or azurite, falcon's eye or laboradite, they are all stones of nobility and indicate a measured response to decision-making. Any issue in your life that falls under the auspices of these stones is one involving principles, nobility of purpose, altruism and a traditional approach. No wonder that, in more chauvinistic times, these were regarded as male stones, for they represent the animus at its most positive and potent: creative blue represents not the assertiveness or sudden surge of the red crystals, but authority and the confidence to take a stand, especially where someone weaker is being treated unjustly.

You may be called upon to arbitrate in a quarrel, perhaps at work, to speak out if you feel strongly about a matter, to take a long-term measured view of any situation and – since this is the colour of leaders – to take the lead or sometimes stand alone over a matter of principle. Long-term gain as opposed to an immediate advantage is usually the best option.

So whatever your age or position, your blue crystal says that you are moving towards a position of personal or professional power, in which you take centre stage, and this can be a great shock for those who see you in the role of friend, mother, wife or compliant colleague. Until now, yours may have been the quiet strength that is sometimes mistaken for acquiescence. Trust your wisdom and take every opportunity to shine or to take control, not least of your own destiny: you can be sure that you will succeed.

You may need to make unpopular decisions. If you have recently been promoted or are enjoying success, the road may seem lonely, and occasionally you may long for anonymity and the approval of your peers. Insecure men may call you power-mad or worse, but that is a compliment, for they are taking you seriously and, at the end of the day, respect is the highest accolade, as it proves you have succeeded through your own merits.

Receptive blue

Aquamarine, blue lace agate, celestite and blue moonstones soften and modify the power of the blue crystal, tempering justice with mercy and melting the rigidity of absolute rights and wrongs with an awareness of motives and human weakness that is very different from deliberate malice. This is the anima face of power that I mentioned in connection with Juno and Minerva. So the receptive blue crystal suggests that you may need to compromise and abide by the spirit rather than the letter of the law where your rights are concerned. You may need to accept that an unfair situation may only be partially resolved, but that any improvement is worthwhile.

These stones may appear when you are in conflict with an authority figure, perhaps an unfair boss, a sniping senior colleague or a cantankerous or disapproving older relative. You need to assert your rights, but in a way that defuses the situation and avoids direct confrontation, which rarely works in these cases. It may take time, and if it is not possible for you to move away from the source of the problem, you may need to tackle each injustice or unfair criticism quietly but with determination each time an incident arises, and so defeat the dragon inch by inch (the receptive green crystals may help).

Remain true to yourself and do not give way on core issues; maintain your integrity, using quiet determination, rather than entering into power games or character assassination, however justifiable. In this way, professional glass ceilings do give way and opposition melts. The fast track is not the only or the most secure route to success, so persevere and you will win through.

Reading two blue stones
Tradition is the issue when both blue crystals are cast in a reading, and a need to look to the past to understand the present and so anticipate future courses. The Vikings believed that our fate was a web of past, present and future, woven by the three Norns, or Fates, and was constantly being torn apart as the interrelation of past and present changed the future. For as soon as we experience a moment, the present becomes the past.

We may talk about walking away from a destructive or redundant situation or relationship and starting again in a new place, in a new career or with a new person. But these dramatic gestures can be superfluous if we carry within us the past, caught in a time bubble; if we do not learn from our mistakes or build on the worthwhile elements of our past, our efforts will be in vain.

Two blue stones can point to the need to avoid repeating past experiences, but are usually far more positive. They indicate that we have within us the wisdom to assimilate what we have learned so far from a variety of sources, personal, familial, formal and informal, and to make decisions, not blindly or impulsively, but by recognising the pattern of events. It may be a time for assessment and reassessment and for taking stock of what has been achieved and the positive aspects of any reversals. The conventional path may be the one to follow for now; so read the contracts, make sure paperwork, especially concerning legal matters, is up to date and consider options and potentialities carefully, so that you move forward from a position of strength and certainty.

Purple crystals

With a creative purple stone in your right hand and a receptive in the left you can access an even deeper wisdom than that contained in the blue stones; listen to what some call the *wise ancestors*, the *tribal voice* or Jung's *collective unconscious*, the *anima mundi* of the Platonic philosophers. Here Jupiter assumes the robes of the priest and spiritual leader rather than of emperor or earthly ruler. Purple was also the colour of the ancient Egyptian god Osiris, one of the archetypal sacrifice deities found in mythology from early times, who died that the Sun might be reborn and the crops would grow each year. So purple stones are very special and are concerned with your spiritual and psychic rather than material development. If you are only buying one stone at first, pick the receptive purple stone as this is the key one.

Reading purple crystals

Creative purple

You may have chosen lapis lazuli, the 'eye of the gods', sodalite or sugilite, all of which represent a deep level of spirituality. For these are the stones of the seekers after truth, and however happy or successful you may be, these stones are a reminder that there is always something more, which can be experienced as an intangible yearning when you stand by the ocean or see a magnificent sunset.

You may be questioning the meaning and purpose of your life and seeking fulfilment in a more spiritual or creative way. The most successful woman can suddenly realise that cumulus clouds are making meaningful pictures in the sky outside the office window or the rustling leaves are offering profound messages in the dingiest square, as they have done for thousands of years; it is at such moments that she is aware that an older, deeper part of herself is slowly evolving.

Creative purple crystals can be a call to develop your innate psychic or healing abilities or to rise above any pettiness that may surround you at home or work. Here may be a choice between physical gratification or material advantage and spiritual satisfaction. You may connect with your Higher Self, with angelic or spirit guardians, or you may receive answers from a source of knowledge you did not know you possessed. Some believe that we are tapping the abilities of our 'other brain' that the conscious mind holds in check, the seat of the soul and the essential self that survives after death.

Receptive purple

These crystals include amethyst, which is used for cleansing other crystals and is a prime healing and calming stone, together with kunzite and fluorite. These are the crystals of rest and calm sleep, of withdrawal from the material world and its demands to the inner world of dreams, daydreams and waking visions, to spontaneous meditative states where insights flow unbidden and the limitations of time and space have little significance. You may be feeling stressed or exhausted, or experiencing a difficult period or ending, and need time to gain the strength to move forward.

Or you may find that activities and commitments that began as pleasure have now become a chore and you long only to be still, to be and not to do (there are close links with the black receptive crystals). Modern women try to work, care for a home, be scintillating companions and passionate lovers, work out at the gym and take a home course in economics, and then they wonder why they are drained of energy, have minor accidents or suffer a succession of colds. It is at these times that the gentle purple crystals will suggest a creative withdrawal until energy flows again.

Reading two purple stones

Your purple stones are the psychic stones and may represent a leap into the unknown or an awareness that there is light at the end of the tunnel – this in a sense takes us back to the beginning and the white crystals.

When you cast both types of purple stone, there may be an important decision to make and no clear pointers or conflicting advice from experts and friends alike. At such times you have to dip deep into the hidden well of wisdom, perhaps through meditation on your purple stones or by charting your daily selection of crystals during the crucial period. Light candles and look deep into your divinatory purple stones or perhaps a large piece of uncut amethyst.

Perhaps the answer will come in your dreams, especially if you sleep with both purple stones beneath your pillow after the reading and light lavender incense to fragrance your bedroom before going to sleep. You know that there are no assurances at this point, but you are not alone – you have your inner star to guide you and hopefully your guardian angel to save you if you stumble.

DAY 17
A nine-day reading

For this reading, you will use one crystal selected on each of nine days. I suggested earlier in the book that it might be helpful to keep a record in your crystal journal to see whether any crystals appeared regularly, indicating that a particular strength was needed in your life or a predominance in some area. You need a period of about nine days to register a pattern, although some people prefer to carry out a weekly review, perhaps on a Sunday morning or evening, as a means of assessing the week and planning the one ahead. Either way, your crystals may reflect a period of calm rather than a need for change, and this can be a reassurance that your life is on course.

Julia's reading

Julia is single, in her thirties, and lives a lakeside trailer near San Francisco. She was contemplating whether to pay the increased rent demanded when the lease came up for renewal, which would drain all her resources. Alternatively, she could move back to the city and share an apartment, which would also cut down on the costs and frustrations of commuting.

Julia cast the following crystals over nine days from her full 20 stones:

Day 1 A receptive blue stone: a blue lace agate.

Day 2 A creative purple stone: a lapis lazuli.

Day 3 A creative purple stone: a lapis lazuli.

Day 4 A receptive white stone: a moonstone.

Day 5 A creative green stone: an aventurine.

Day 6 A receptive blue stone: a blue lace agate.

Day 7 A receptive purple stone: an amethyst.

Day 8 A creative purple stone: a lapis lazuli.

Day 9 A creative red stone: a garnet.

Julia had a significant amount of repetition in the crystals she selected over the nine days and chose more creative than receptive stones, suggesting that the way ahead lay in immediate change and action rather than letting events take their course.

Days 1 and 6: Receptive blue

This is the stone of compromise and also of dealing with difficult authority figures. The owner of the trailer park had been increasing the rent over the period of years she had been living there and had imposed an increasing number of restrictions. But Julia did have occupancy rights and so could use these to negotiate a fairer price than the one asked if she wished to stay.

Days 2, 3 and 8: Creative purple

What did Julia really want? The creative purple suggests the peace and beauty of lakeside life with its abundant wildlife and closeness to the changing seasons. City life was increasingly filling her with a sense of emptiness and alienation, though she was good at her work managing a small bookstore specialising in rare volumes.

Day 4: Receptive white

This heralded a new beginning, which together with the creative purple crystal suggested spiritual rather than material fulfilment. So that would not indicate a return to full-time city life.

Day 5: Creative green

This echoed the creative purple stones. If Julia were to follow her heart, she said there would be no question: she would live full-time in her trailer and concentrate on the wildlife paintings she had recently started to sell. But how could this be achieved financially, especially with the rent increase that would demand she spent even longer in the city, working evenings in one of the main branches of a bookstore chain?

Day 7: Receptive purple

This had double significance. It spoke of the need for Julia to withdraw from the stresses and rely on her inner world – another indication that it was right to remain where she was happy and if possible spend even more time there. The double purple, the inspirational factor, offered the answer. The position of warden of the trailer park was about to become vacant because the present warden's wife was pregnant and so they could no longer manage on his relatively low wage. Could Julie give up the bookstore job, with its possibility of later promotion, and live full-time at the lakeside, developing her art work to supplement her income? She would have free rent and site fees. But she would have to persuade the very difficult and chauvinistic site owner to let her take over – back to the compromise of the receptive blue.

Day 9: Creative red

Like the good fairy, this gave Julie the confidence to approach the site owner with her proposals for attracting the holiday trade. Her sales skills came to the fore.

As a result of her application and perseverance, she is now on three months' trial at the site and has started to sell a number of her paintings.

Often opportunities do exist but we feel that they are not for us, or we lack the confidence to make that leap in the dark. The crystals confirm underlying strengths and push us towards chances and openings we might have missed. Julia is taking a risk, but has the joy of her surroundings and is prepared, if necessary, to look for a new job in the city if it all falls through.

Pink crystals

Hold a creative pink crystal in your right hand and a receptive one in your left and you will experience warmth, tranquillity and stillness as racing thoughts and anxieties fade away. For these are the stones of Venus in her gentler aspect and encompass affection, romance, friendship, reconciliation and harmony. Pink unites red, the colour with the longest wavelength, with violet, the colour with the shortest wavelength, so tempering power and action with spirituality and understanding. Pink crystals are not weak, sentimental or 'girly': they are the balance between logic and emotion and they filter the excesses of both to calm acceptance of life as it is, and offer immunity to the petty irritations that litter the everyday world.

If you are buying only one pink stone, choose a receptive pink as this is the key crystal.

Reading pink crystals

Creative pink

You may choose coral, rhodonite that is sometimes streaked with black, or sugilite. Women are natural peacemakers. Even allowing for the idealisation of distance ages, evidence would suggest that neolithic matriarchal societies who worshipped the Mother Goddess, tended to be driven by the desire not for dominance by conquest, but for alliances and mutual trading. They lived by agriculture rather than hunting and gathering, and so brought a more settled existence. Modern businesswomen at their most positive are usually only ruthless when necessary and not as part of a power game, for women are by nature cultivators rather than hunters. Of course, some women are spiteful or cruel, but dig deep enough and you will often discover that it is buried distress or suffering that has warped the natural flow of love.

These are the crystals of the peacemaker, and you may find yourself reconciling differences between warring relatives, friends or work colleagues, or finding ways to balance conflicting demands in your own life or that of others. This in itself gives you a position of strength. Not only does your positive attitude create a sense of harmony within your own mind, but surveys have demonstrated that those who criticise others become associated themselves with these negative qualities.

You may also need to heal or at least resolve coldness or animosity between yourself and someone in your immediate world. Even if it is not your fault, if you attempt reconciliation, and are rebuffed, then you have freed yourself from the guilt of not trying, for it is not in your nature to live with animosity. Sometimes, however, the breach is too deep or the other person intractable, and all you can do is to offer the hand of friendship or love – and then move on.

On the other hand, your stone may point to a new relationship of love or friendship, which, if you allow it to unfold slowly, will bring happiness and the growth of trust following a hurt or betrayal in a previous relationship.

Vulnerability is not the same as weakness, and while it is important for women to protect themselves from unnecessary malice or pain, female compassion is a quality that grows with experience, and so this is a stone that grows in power and intensity over the years. A woman beginning a new relationship in her fifties or sixties or even in old age is just as sensitive as a young woman embarking on her first serious love affair. This vulnerability does not diminish, for it is at the wellspring of womanhood, but life's sorrows and joys do bring wisdom and understanding of the human condition, and so love and deep friendships in the later years can be the richest of all.

Receptive pink

Rose quartz, like amethyst, is a stone of healing, especially for children and animals. You may also use pink beryl, kunzite or tourmaline or discover a matt pink stone, a pink and white-flecked granite or pink sandstone on a happy day in the countryside. These natural Earth stones contain grounding powers that can be of great value as your psychic abilities unfold.

These are the crystals of reconciliation within yourself. Frequently receptive pink stones are cast outside the circles into the area of Fate, for women are good at caring for others but may fail to listen to their own needs and blame themselves for the unhappiness of those around them. 'I can't forgive myself' and 'I should have done something to help' are words that have passed my own lips when I have been unable to protect those I love, sometimes from situations of their own making. Other women for whom I have given crystal readings carry similar, sometimes unnecessary burdens of guilt over omissions that are justifiable when you put your own needs first.

Perhaps an overgrown baby bird tried to fly at long last and fell; or you were unable to help out a colleague or friend because you were too busy, refused to lend money to someone who lurches from one crisis to another but never pays you back, or chose a weekend with a lover rather than visiting your mother.

Perhaps you have placed yourself for too long between warring relatives, friends or people at work who have taken out their anger on you rather than each other. As more families are split by divorce and separation, a mother may find herself acting as a wedge between a child and a new partner or two sets of children, and still end up as the villain – ironically, removing the need for the combatants to learn to live together. Siblings of any age can compete for attention quite ruthlessly.

Many a woman has intervened in the troubles between her lover and his mother, only to have both turn on her. For they may have been playing this game for years and invariably turn the rescuer into the dragon. I have had my own fingers burned more than once, protecting a man from a mother who was haranguing or criticising him, only to find that both were unconsciously conspiring to fulfil a familiar, hidden agenda and deeply resented my intrusion.

So it may be time to step back from stage-managing your unruly players – and try practising a soliloquy or two. Equally, if you arrive in a new workplace that is split into factions, it may be the way that equilibrium is customarily maintained, so wait and observe before marching in with the flag of peace.

Reading two pink stones

If you get both kinds of pink stone in a reading, then the theme is harmony, bringing you peace of mind that is partly achieved by avoiding the hazards inherent in the pink receptive stones. But it is much more: it is the innermost centre of tranquillity, what T.S. Eliot called 'the still point of the turning world' in his poem *The Four Quartets*. He also described this state as 'the stillness between two waves'. It is achieved by balancing the needs of self and others, of reason and intuition, assertiveness and receptivity, material and spiritual needs, of commitment and the separate self, so that like a see-saw each of these qualities can rise to the fore when needed, then sit back again, restoring the balance.

I talked in the section on purple stones of the Chinese philosophy of Taoism. I mentioned the concept was that of extremes and how it is believed that extreme *yang*, power of action, automatically becomes *yin*, receptivity and inaction and vice versa. But though all life is changing and we cannot hold back the moments, some philosophies, such as Buddhism, believe that we need to reach a state where we can step off the wheel of change and existence into the still centre that is beyond inner or external turmoil, and it is this centre that is the key to true bliss and immortality.

For many of us such states are far off and spiritual detachment from earthly matters and human emotions is confined to moments of meditation, or those spontaneous 'peak experiences' as the psychologist Abraham Maslow called them, when we do momentarily connect with the harmony of the universe.

But the two pink crystals are perhaps the most fortunate of colour combinations, indicating that your inner and outer worlds are in harmony and that any disruption around you is only temporary and not serious. You are on the right track and should not let anyone tell you otherwise. Stop on a traffic island and let the discordant noises merge into harmony, focus mentally on a field of flowers as your crowded train lurches to a halt halfway to work, and you will arrive at your destination able to cope with anything.

DAY 19
Brown crystals

As you hold your brown creative crystal in your right hand and your receptive in the left, you make connection with the Earth beneath your feet and the reassuring protection of the Earth Mother. Your green crystals of growth, especially jade and moss agate, made a similar connection. Brown crystals are the stones of the Mother Goddess. The earliest Mother Goddess statuettes, for example the Venus of Willendorf which dates from around 24000–22000 BC, were placed in the earth and perhaps carried from place to place as early tribes followed the hunt.

Reading brown crystals

Brown is the colour of the earth and can vary surprisingly in both vibrancy and hue – look at a ploughed field in the sunlight or a field of ripening corn. Brown crystals, too, reflect this variance and richness. They are the stones that indicate our homes and domestic life – the first houses were created in the rocks – and also all practical matters, money and a step-by-step approach to any project.

If you are only buying one brown stone initially, choose the receptive version as this is the key stone.

Creative brown

You may select an agate, a jasper or tiger's eye, stones of strength that assure you that any venture, especially concerning your home, finances or business matters, has firm foundations. While there may not be immediate results or rapid returns, in the long torm you will succeed. These are crystals of patience and perseverance, of the slower path that connects you at every stage with your roots, your innate wisdom and the ultimate purpose of your journey, of which you rarely lose sight. They may reflect a quiet but contented period in your life, of stability and security in the most positive sense, or rebuilding after loss.

These are the building block crystals, whether you seek ultimately to build a financial empire or a secure, happy home for yourself alone or with a family. All creatures need a base from which to roam. The Vikings would float the wooden door pillars of their homesteads whenever they approached new shores – and wherever the pillars landed, they would create their first resting place on the foreign shore.

Perhaps you seek practical improvements in your home or you are looking for a change of residence, to build or rebuild your finances, to learn new but related skills. Whatever the area of your life, any progress should be made within the context of your present situation – moves tend to be across town rather than to another country or continent. Those greater changes reside with the more mercurial yellow crystals.

You are a natural creator of order and beauty and you may be concerned with environmental issues, especially in your own area: you are the one who has plans for the waste ground that could be made into a herb garden or play area; you are concerned about food or water pollution or deforestation. Your strong practical streak means that any campaigns you pursue will be well planned, and for this reason you are a formidable opponent in ensuring that fine words are followed by action. You may be especially concerned with animal conservation – material benefits are for you only a means to an end.

If your aims are realistic and moderate – moderation is the key of creative brown crystals – success is assured. Break down your long-term projects into stages and persevere until your dreams take on tangible form.

Receptive brown

These stones include desert rose, leopardskin or snakeskin jasper and rutilated quartz, all of which contain inner treasure. These final stones are for me the most precious and are not at all dull or static. Indeed they represent the potential fruit, tree or flower that lies within every kernel or seed; they urge you to shed what is burdening you as a snake sheds its skin in the spring. I have in my own collection matt, brown-stained limestones, containing fossils and brown flint, which I found on a beach where dinosaur footprints can still be detected in the rocks.

When you cast or select a receptive brown stone, it indicates that you may be feeling overwhelmed by the sheer logistics of your life and are exhausted with juggling the practical demands of work and home commitments. You may be worried about money, or drained by the constant financial demands of dependants. Mothers are increasingly expected to welcome home adult children who have suffered a broken relationship, perhaps with a young child to care for too. The worldwide recession has also led to widespread redundancies, especially among people in their forties and fifties who have little chance of finding another job of similar status. Even formerly safe professions no longer offer a job for life.

Women can be hard hit if they are single and find themselves suddenly unemployed with high mortgages and loans, and if they are married they may find themselves the sole wage-earner in areas of high industrial unemployment. Whether single, in relationships or with partners, they can suddenly find themselves financially or practically responsible for the care of an elderly parent.

But sometimes we do more than our share financially and practically; we clear up after able-bodied families out of a misplaced sense of guilt that goes back generations, rooted in the belief that it is a woman's job to keep a comfortable home. Logic does not enter into it as we move into overdrive, subsidising older children who use their grants and wages as spending money and accept free laundry and room service. Partners, colleagues at work and bosses are all experts at manipulating the guilt strings of a potential carer.

When a senior partner of a firm of solicitors told me she was scrubbing her bathroom at 6 a.m. because her domestic help was due, I realised that this condition knows no boundaries.

So if you are feeling exhausted, step back, delegate, and lock away your cheque book when predators approach with their tales of woe. Personally, I am not much further along this road than I was ten years ago when I first wrote on this topic. But all is not doom and gloom for, as I said, these stones contain hidden treasure – the potential to touch base, reorganise your priorities and above all to turn nurturing energies upon yourself. Give time, love and practical care to *your own* well-being, treat *yourself* as you would your nearest and dearest and each day take a step towards fulfilling *your own* special dreams.

Reading two brown stones
The Earth, when seen from space, is a beautiful blue and has from the earliest periods been associated with the Mother Goddess and all her bounties. Demeter, the Greek corn goddess, was a symbol of the fertility of the land. Roman women held a week-long spring festival in her honour; they called her Ceres. Men were excluded and during the festival participants would eat only products directly harvested from the earth.

The Greek Elusian mysteries too were centred around the rituals of death and rebirth as Demeter's daughter Kore (or Persephone) was stolen by Hades, god of the underworld, and her grief was such that it brought about winter. The return of Persephone for six months of the year allowed spring and summer to bring forth their bounty.

And so the brown stones are symbols of abundance and are connected with the cycle of the seasons. These stones say that there is a time for sowing the seeds of future abundance, of tending the growing crops and of waiting for a relationship or project to mature. Abundance will be yours in its own time if you seek fertility. This can be in the sense of wanting a child, or making an idea or project take root, setting up a money-making scheme or any other practical venture from home improvements to learning a new skill. It is pointless to fret or to take short cuts and anxiety can block all kinds of fertility. Finally, these are the stones of generosity – under the law of magic, whatever you give freely and with love will be returned threefold.

A circle reading with nine stones

Now that you have learned the meanings of all 20 crystals, you can carry out circle readings for others as well as yourself. The cast of nine crystals is especially useful for a major decision or a life review, and you should set aside at least an hour for such a session.

You may wish to light purple or white candles and a divinatory incense, such as sandalwood or frankincense, after taking a relaxing bath to which a few drops of lavender or rose essential oil have been added.

Prepare a simple meal for afterwards, whether you are alone or reading for a friend. 'Cakes and ale' form an essential part of any formal magical ceremony as a way of absorbing the magical energies. Even informally, taking food and drink after a reading, while listening to music by candlelight, can help to make the transition back to the everyday world.

You may find it easier to select your crystals as three groups of three, casting them as three groups and seeing the interactions building up, but if you prefer, select and cast the stones singly.

Wait until all nine crystals are on the cloth, so that you can see the patterns they make and the relative significance of each area of the cloth.

Read the stones in the order they fell, noting clusters or any crystals that cover or displace others.

Miranda's cast of nine

Miranda is about to leave her English-speaking school near Malaga in Spain. Her father works in the export trade and her mother runs a pottery store, specialising in the local ceramics. The whole family speaks fluent Spanish and plays a full part in the life of the village in which they live. Miranda has a place at university back in England, but her boyfriend and many of her friends are Spaniards and she has been offered training as a junior manager at the local sports and music store. Her parents are horrified and point out that in spite of apparent greater freedom, Spanish women are still at a disadvantage in what is basically a deeply male-centred society. They point to the sacrifices they have made to pay for Miranda's schooling and say that she will regret not pursuing her education.

Miranda has temporarily moved into her boyfriend's home, but feels very isolated, and finds she is constantly chaperoned by the older female relatives and that her formerly attentive boyfriend spends his evenings when he is not working with his brothers and cousins at the local bar. But to return home would be to admit defeat and her parents are adamant that she must go to university.

Miranda casts:

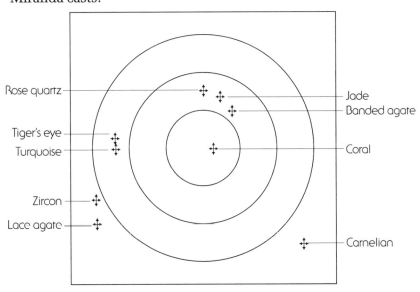

1 **A receptive pink crystal:** a rose quartz in her circle of the inner world.

2 **A creative brown crystal:** a tiger's eye in her circle of action and interaction.

3 **A creative blue crystal:** a turquoise, also in her circle of action and interaction, touching the previous crystal.

4 **A receptive yellow crystal:** a zircon that displaces the previous crystal and landed in the realm of Fate.

5 **A creative pink crystal:** coral that falls in the circle of her essential self.

6 **A receptive green crystal:** a jade, in the circle of her inner world, close to stone 1.

7 **A receptive orange crystal:** a banded agate, in the circle of her inner world, close to stones 1 and 6.

8 **A receptive blue crystal:** a blue lace agate, in the realm of Fate, that displaces the yellow receptive crystal.

9 **A creative orange crystal:** a carnelian, also in the realm of Fate, but on the opposite side from the other two crystals.

Interpreting the crystals

Before you read Miranda's view of the crystals, act as though you were giving the reading and note your responses. If they differ from Miranda's, that is because we each bring our unique world view to the stones and, had it been an actual session, you would have interacted with Miranda and perhaps enabled her to reach even more precise insights.

The reading had slightly more receptive than creative stones, reflecting the number of powerful influences on Miranda that have made her feel she was not mistress of her own fate.

Though usually you would read the stones in the order cast, if there are a lot of interconnections, you my find it easier to interpret the crystals according to the areas in which they fall. This was the method used by Miranda – my own input was minimal.

The circle of the essential self

This is relatively empty as Miranda moves from her younger to adult self. The **creative pink** crystal indicates that Miranda is a natural peacemaker and has found it hard to initiate conflict. She says that for years she has acted as mediator in her parents' tempestuous marriage – this is echoed in the receptive pink crystal. It was her father who was eager for her to go to university in England while her mother was eager for her to attend a Spanish university so that she could still come home at weekends. Her parents were united only in their dislike of her boyfriend and her wish to get a job.

The circle of the inner world

It is in this area that the conflicting demands of others and their effects on Miranda are felt most keenly and where she needs to resolve her feelings in order to make positive decisions about her own future. Here there are three receptive stones: pink, green and orange.

The **receptive pink crystal** speaks of her guilt over the unhappiness of others caused by her decision – she moved away rather than be the centre of conflict. However, Miranda says, nothing has been resolved as she carries guilt within her, illogically she admits, for failing to make her parents' marriage happy.

The **receptive green crystal** talks of being aware of what is going on beneath the surface and listening to our hearts and feelings, allowing the extremes of emotion to settle. In a sense that is what has been happening at Miranda's boyfriend's home where she has been helping in the family café and living a traditional Spanish family life in which she has spent less time with her boyfriend than when she lived at home. This has helped her to see that his restrictive way of life is not for her.

The **receptive orange crystal** highlights her sense of lack of identity, living in the shadow of first her own family and now her boyfriend's, which proved not to be a road to freedom after all.

The circle of action and interaction

Here there are two creative stones that are closely linked, brown and blue. The **creative brown** talks of practical or financial steps towards a realistic future with a firm foundation close to home. Miranda took this to confirm that she should go ahead with her plan to take the job she had been offered in the music store that would lead to work in other branches throughout Spain if she did well. But what of her domestic arrangements? The **blue** power stone gave her the clue, indicating that she should claim her personal power and have the confidence to stand up for what she wanted.

Miranda realised that she did not want to spend her future with her boyfriend and that her intense love for him had been partly her way of rebelling because her parents were so adamant that she should not become involved. If she took the job, she would earn enough to rent a small apartment and for the first time to shape her own destiny. Her future in-laws had been hinting about weddings and babies, the latter of which she did not want for years, if ever.

The realm of Fate

With so much uncertainty surrounding Miranda, it is not surprising that there are three crystals here: receptive yellow, which displaced the creative blue stone, receptive blue, and a creative orange on the other side from the other two. Receptive yellow talks about lack of communication and so Miranda needs to explain to her parents, her boyfriend and her boyfriend's family how she feels and what she intends to do. This will not be easy, but it is the only way to move forward.

The **receptive blue crystal** tends to appear when the subject is in conflict with an authority figure and so Miranda needs to defuse the situation with her parents without capitulating.

Finally, the **creative orange** indicates a new emerging identity that can develop as she takes control of her own destiny.

What of the doubling effect? Two pink stones focus on Miranda's own inner harmony that will increase as she no longer accepts responsibility for her parents' happiness. The orange crystals concentrate on the area of boundaries.

Miranda felt she could only break away from her parents by physically moving away. But she does love them and wants them to be part of her life, without dictating its course. The two blue stones indicate that our present and future are linked with our past, enabling Miranda to build on what was good in her home life and education, and her experiences of living and working with a traditional Spanish family.

She knows that in spite of his modern appearance and liberated words, her boyfriend at heart wants a wife to stay at home with the women. Some Spaniards, especially those brought up in the city, are liberated and accept wives who are as free as they are. But many do still want a woman who will become part of the extended family and will understand their way of life, which includes their socialising with male relatives rather than with their womenfolk.

A meditative reading

I have suggested that when you are reading crystals you begin by holding each crystal and allowing impressions to form. This activates the visual part of the brain that links with the timeless universal symbols or *archetypes* of mankind. The concept of archetypes has been likened to the dream symbols of the collective or tribal mind. Just as dream symbols access the depths of our personal mind, so do crystals, runes and Tarot cards (all of which feature in the *Talk to the Woman Within* series) offer a doorway into the greater collective memory bank of experience. Through our crystal work we can reach higher levels of awareness or consciousness.

This is not at all fanciful. Picture a moment in your life when sudden awareness overrides the automatic level of functioning that characterises much of our waking life. You look up and see the Sun filtering through leaves in a forest, a sky filled with stars or the Full Moon over water. Suddenly everyday concerns fall away, you are overwhelmed by the sheer beauty and wonder, and in a sense you become momentarily part of what was described in the world of Ancient Greece as the 'harmony of the spheres'. You are the stars, the sunlight and the leaves all at the same time and yet are still yourself. Remember the magic of childhood when anything was possible? We held the secrets of the universe, but lacked the maturity to understand them.

These higher levels of awareness can be reached in a state of meditation, using your divinatory crystals as a powerful focus. We can all meditate. It is the natural state experienced when you gaze into a fountain, or the embers of a dying fire – or even the glowing barbecue coals as evening falls. Candles are especially evocative for meditative states.

Preparing for crystal meditation

The following ritual can be carried out whenever you do not have a specific question or decision to be made and is an important stage in developing your natural psychic awareness. You may, however, discover answers to questions you had not realised you needed to ask.

✛ Begin by making a circle of 14 crystals on a table, starting with the creative red crystal, followed by receptive red, creative orange, followed by receptive orange, and then the pairs of yellow, green, blue, purple and finally pink. Leave spaces between them.

✛ In the centre, place your two white crystals; they should be touching, as white is the synthesis of all other colours. The darker colours of brown and black are not so effective for meditation, but place these crystals, two on each side of you, for grounding.

✛ Behind each creative crystal light a small candle of the same colour with a larger white one in the centre of the circle. You can use small metal dishes if you do not have enough holders, but make sure each is sufficiently deep so that the wax will not spill on the table.

Beginning your crystal meditation

Make sure that your candles are in a safe place. Sleep is a common result of meditation so ensure that your candles cannot be knocked over and cause a fire or burn you, should you drift off. Small candles in enclosed glass holders or even differently coloured nightlights are safe forms of candle magic. You can even place your crystals in the bottom of a large crystal bowl and float appropriately coloured candles on the surface. Another choice, if you have a hearth with a grate, the magical and spiritual centre of homes in earlier times, is to put your crystals and candles on a metal tray within the fireplace and sit on cushions, well back from the enclosed hearth.

✢ Choose a time when you are not too tired; have a bath in a gentle fragrance such as geranium or chamomile, followed by a very simple meal or warm drink, as you may be too sleepy afterwards.

✢ Wear something loose and light and sit where you can gaze into the candle flame safely.

✢ Light the candles clockwise, beginning with the white candle, followed by the red, and when you have done so, invoke psychic protection, perhaps focusing on four of the candles at intervals around the circle as your candle guardians. Switch off all other lights.

✢ Place both feet flat on the floor. If you wish, support your back with a pillow or sit in a chair with arm rests for your elbows.

✢ Sit up straight without straining your muscles. Experiment with different tables and distances until you feel comfortable.

✢ In the sitting position, you should have your arms resting comfortably in your lap with palms upwards. Comfort is the essence of good meditation.

✢ Some people prefer to sit cross-legged on the floor or cushions with their hands supporting their knees (use a low table or the hearth for your candles).

✢ Aim initially for five, then ten minutes of meditation, building up to 20–30 minutes; be ruled by your own needs.

✢ Do not fight the sensation of the outer world returning, even if this happens before you had expected your meditation to end; this means your psyche has done its work.

Breathing in the light

✢ Visualise all the coloured rays from the different crystals, amplified by the candlelight, pouring into the central white crystals and these being synthesised into an arc of white light. Some people perceive this synthesised light as golden.

+ See yourself surrounded by a circle of pure light, emanating from your candle and white crystals in the centre.

+ Let this circle expand until you are bathed in it, but can see quite clearly through it to the separate beams of coloured light that form the spokes of a wheel around the white or golden centre.

+ Concentrate on breathing, slowly and deeply. Take a slow, deep breath through your nose, hold it while you count, one, two, three, and slowly exhale through your mouth.

+ As you inhale, visualise the pure white or golden light entering your body and dark light leaving. Continue until you see only the white or golden light being inhaled and exhaled, and your breathing is slow and steady.

Entering the light

+ Become your breathing and do not attempt to move beyond it, remaining focused on the wheel of crystals and candlelight; do not attempt to see any pictures, although some people report seeing sparks emanating from the candles at this stage.

+ As you gaze, blinking whenever you need to, gradually all other sights, sounds and sensations will merge and recede, leaving you in the stillness of the light.

+ You may find that one particular crystal may act as the focus, and this may vary from meditation to meditation.

+ If you move your gaze from the central crystal and light to the whole wheel, this will happen quite spontaneously and all the other lights will merge into the background of your chosen colour as though your psychic camera was zooming in on this particular aspect. At other times, the whole wheel may be the focus. Allow any words and pictures also to come and go without attempting to hold or analyse them.

+ Gradually you will find that you are moving away from the focus, connecting with your breathing once more and seeing the light also fade. As you do this, external sounds will return and your normal range of vision will expand until you are fully aware once more.

✢ Stretch like a cat, slowly and luxuriantly, and spend the time before sleep listening to gentle music, or perhaps the sound of a rainforest or ocean. Some people use music for the whole meditation. I have suggested sources for music in the addresses section on pages 156–7.

✢ If you received any inspirations or images during your meditation, record them in words or pictures.

✢ If the candles are still burning at bedtime, blow them out, sending the light to those you love, not forgetting yourself. Place the crystal that became the centre of your meditation beneath your pillow and your dreams may continue the theme of your experience.

Adding to your divinatory set

I have about 150 small crystals in my divinatory set that I have collected since 1994 (I lost my originals in the Los Angeles earthquake). These crystals I have bought on special days out or have been given by my children and friends. I am convinced that there is a cosmic crystal exchange system. I frequently give one of my crystals that seems of special significance to people for whom I read, because a crystal given in love or friendship is ten times more potent than one you buy. I also offer crystals with specific healing or magical properties, for example an amethyst to someone with a headache or a rose quartz to a person facing a confrontation or stressful interview or test. Invariably, soon afterwards, I am given a crystal or I find one that addresses my current need.

I have discovered that no matter whether you use 20 or 200 crystals, they are the relevant crystals. To give just one example, Jess, a 60-year-old market gardener, who was overwhelmed by the return home of her daughter and three children to her mobile home on her smallholding, picked six matt brown crystals apparently at random from my bag and was amazed at the rainbow hues of the remaining crystals when she looked in the bag afterwards.

Because the system does not operate on random selection but on psychokinetic principles, whereby you select the crystal colours and types you need, as long as you add crystals to your divinatory set in pairs, one creative for one receptive, the system still works. You do not even need to add crystals of the same colour.

Some people prefer to use only their 20 basic crystals for divination or healing and may substitute different ones so that their set becomes right for them. You do not need to use a larger set unless you wish to. You can select your set for divination according to your personal preference and keep any extra crystals in your special place for scrying, for psychometry or for meditation.

In my original list on Day 1, I listed three or four alternatives for each colour and so there is already a wide selection of crystals you can add to your collection. You can also buy different shades of your divinatory crystals that will register subtly different energies. For example, I have many banded agates in my set that contain different intensities and combinations of colours. If you buy a crystal and cannot find the properties for it either in this book or the ones I suggest in the booklist on page 154, hold it in your cupped hands, close your eyes and let its properties unfold through your different senses.

The following crystals are those that I have found especially potent for divination and healing. They are listed in alphabetical order. Choose individual examples that are rounded and smooth to touch, and avoid those that seem brittle or sharp, which may scratch your other crystals. You can usually buy even striated crystals in a polished form.

Alexandrite (creative)
Colours: Clear violet or green, light blue or orange-yellow iridescence.
Qualities: Releases energies and overcomes mental and spiritual as well as physical energy blockages. For all forms of healing and for increasing self-esteem, alexandrite assists connection with the Higher Self and increases psychic awareness. A bringer of joy.

Danburite (creative)
Colours: Clear crystal.
Qualities: Radiates pure, white light and the Life Force, illuminating body, mind and spirit; encourages truth, openness to the cosmos and loving relationships; strengthens the mind. It is a powerful healer.

Dioptase (receptive)
Colours: Green or deep blue-green translucent to transparent crystals.

Qualities: Removes lingering negativity, heals sadness, heartache and loss, encourages self-love. Empowers the wearer with courage and the ability to love unconditionally and to accept abundance from all sources; also for healing the Earth.

Elestial (creative)
Colours: A form of clear or smoky quartz.
Qualities: Known as the 'All-seeing', a bringer of joy and light. Removes confusion and illusion and offers a wider perspective on any situation: opens psychic channels for spiritual evolution and to enable the user to see beyond the material and immediate world. Initially elestial may intensify self-doubt, so carry it for a while before using it for divination.

Fuchsite (receptive)
Colours: Light green.
Qualities: Promotes happiness, laughter and friendship; aids recovery from depression.

Obsidian (receptive)
Colours: Translucent black to dark smoky grey; absorbs dark and converts to white light, reflecting light through it.
Qualities: Objectivity, earthing; antidote to illusion and escapism. Absorbs and dissolves anger, criticism, fears. Protects sensitive people from negativity, helps the user to release regrets for lost love; a good crystal for beginners to use. Brings light-giving energy to harness basic instincts for higher purposes; encourages flexibility and change. A stone for travellers; strengthens prophetic and predictive abilities, especially when held up to the light for scrying and meditation.

Snowflake obsidian (receptive)
Colour: Black with white spots.
Qualities: Assists clairaudience; also acceptance of our shadow side and basic instincts as part of whole self, but may initially amplify this side, so should be carried before divinatory uses. An excellent stone for endings that take time and gradually allow the first steps to new beginnings.

Black onyx (creative)
Qualities: All colours of onyx balance and calm intense mood swings and emotions. Black onyx in particular has earthing powers; even in Christian times, the head of Mars for courage or Hercules for strength would be engraved on black onyx; also offers protection against foes of all kinds, and in conflict situations quells anger and spite. Helps to change bad habits. Black onyx is always dyed, but is nevertheless a powerful divinatory stone.

Blue onyx (creative)
Qualities: For saying what needs to be said; the more translucent or clear stones are more potent.

Green onyx (receptive)
Qualities: Balances emotions and enables the user to detect sincerity in others.

Yellow onyx (creative)
Qualities: Encourages logical processes.

Opal (receptive)
Colours: Iridescent white, cream, fire and black.
Qualities: Not easy to find the right shape for divination, but worth persevering. Sometimes one that has been set in a ring but has fallen out is suitable. Excellent for meditation, psychometry and scrying.

Known as the 'rainbow stone', its name comes from *upala*, Sanskrit for 'precious stone'. In China opals were considered living gems because the hue of an opal could change so rapidly.

Because it contains water, it is a stone closely linked with the emotions of the user; it amplifies and mirrors feelings, especially buried ones. Opal will change colour according to the mood of the wearer or according to energy levels, and absorbs and retains emotions and thoughts. Because of this it is a difficult stone to pass on and so undeservedly has the reputation of being unlucky. Opal also increases awareness of possibilities; offers alternatives not considered consciously when one is trapped in a situation. Offers protection against the anger and negativity of others.

Black opal (receptive)
Qualities: Links with the soul; helps one see one's potential; enhances divination, access to past lives and astral travel.

Dark-blue opal (creative)
Qualities: A very powerful opal, one of the most potent, prompting words spoken from the heart.

Fire opal (creative)
Qualities: So called because of their iridescent flashes of red and blue light, fire opals are good for sexual problems, especially in women, and for financial acumen. A stone of love and passion.

Water opal (receptive)
Qualities: Clear and colourless, but in the light displays iridescent colours inside; a special stone for scrying.

White opal (creative)
Qualities: Balances the two hemispheres of the brain so that reason and intuition are complementary, not opposites.

Peridot (creative)
Colours: Clear, bright green or green-yellow; a transparent form of olivine.
Qualities: Traditionally believed by the ancient Egyptians, Aztecs and Incas to heal the heart, peridot attracts prosperity, aids personal growth and brings new perspectives; good for developing and maintaining good relationships, alleviating jealousy, depression, anger, fear and anxiety; enhances mental clarity and patience and encourages a positive emotional outlook. Strengthens the Life Force.

Pyrite/fool's gold (receptive)
Colour: Dark, rock-like with gold inclusions.
Qualities: A stone of the Sun, said to be a reminder to avoid illusion and the easy path. A powerful earthing stone, especially

after divination or meditation; provides focus and logic, improves memory, clears confused thoughts and indecision and eases anxiety, frustration and depression. A natural money magnet. Pyrite is brittle so should be handled with care, kept separately when not in use, and not washed. You will need to find a suitable shape for divination, but it is well worth having as an additional stone.

Rubellite/red tourmaline (creative)
Colours: Red or pink.
Qualities: Strengthens mind and body; gives new hope, courage, energy, stamina and also persistence. A stone of fertility and endurance.

Selenite (creative)
Colours: White or clear striated crystals, transparent to translucent.
Qualities: Mental focus, emotional and intellectual growth, strengthens survival instincts. Traditionally a repository for human experience and history. Transmits white light and energy of Higher Consciousness through the whole body; increases awareness of different dimensions. Assists in leaving behind destructive and outworn relationships and situations. A crystal that can heal the Earth.

Spinel (creative)
Colours: Transparent, colourless (pure form), black, blue, green, purple, pink.
Qualities: Alleviates stress and depression. Aids mental rejuvenation, especially in colourless form.

Red spinel (creative)
Qualities: Often known as the 'female' ruby, renews strength and stamina, and increases survival instincts.

Tanzanite (receptive)
Colours: Clear, blue, purple, violet.
Qualities: A stone of gentle change, tanzanite uplifts and makes the heart receptive to love. Place on the brow for clairvoyance,

clairaudience, visions, connection to other realms, protection and for bringing thoughts into actuality; also expands the range and focus of physical and mental vision and hearing: especially powerful for meditation and healing visualisation.

Tourmaline (receptive)
Colours: Black, blue, green, pink, watermelon (green, pink and red striped) striated, clear or semi-transparent gem.
Qualities: All tourmalines strengthen the body and spirit, lifting the user from the material to higher plains of awareness. Tourmaline endows protective light on the wearer. Dispels fear, negativity and sorrows, encourages peaceful sleep and eases compulsions.

Black tourmaline
Qualities: Protective against hostile feelings and negative intent. Links higher and lower levels of consciousness, removing fears, resentment, neuroses and obsessions; brings healing powers and psychic insights back to the everyday sphere.

Blue tourmaline
Qualities: Establishes links with Higher Self for divination, psychic work and also for a sense of peace, and clear but tactful communication; fosters patience in a difficult situation.

Green tourmaline
Qualities: Balances emotions so that they do not drain physical energies. Restores enthusiasm and optimism and encourages abundance in all spheres, not least compassion; brings harmony to mind and whole body. Attracts money.

Watermelon tourmaline
Qualities: A stone of balance, also associated with rebirth and renewal. Integrates all that is best in mind, body and spirit in the user for a compassionate, realistic but powerful approach to life.

DAY 23
A joint crystal reading

I discovered joint readings quite by chance when I read the crystals separately for mothers and daughters, pairs of sisters, and husbands and wives at a series of healing festivals in the north of England and noticed that they independently selected either identical or related stones on issues that concerned them both. As a result I began to teach and demonstrate joint readings. They are an excellent way of resolving relationship issues or suggesting new directions in an emotional or business partnership, especially if there is an impasse. You can use this method in your own relationships and partnerships or when reading crystals for others.

✤ Begin by asking the two people to identify an area that they would like to examine. There need not be a specific question, and other related aspects of their lives will naturally appear as crystals are selected.

✤ Rather than casting the crystals on to the cloth, ask each person to select a crystal in turn until six have been chosen. I have found that this is the ideal number for this form of divination.

✤ Each should hold the chosen crystal in turn, beginning with the person who did not select it, and take time to receive and communicate impressions. This joint psychic link is the key to the reading and only after the couple have spoken should you, if you are assisting with interpretation, take the stone and add your impressions.

✤ Interpret each crystal in turn in the order it was cast, allowing the meaning of the whole reading to evolve naturally, rather as though a story was unfolding. The answer that is finally revealed may be to an entirely different but more deep-seated question.

✣ If the reading is your own, you will find that the fresh psychometric impressions of your partner, relation or friend will counterbalance your own knowledge of the stones. Suspend judgement and allow the crystals to be your guide and they will offer unexpected solutions, even to well trodden avenues of contention.

✣ When reading for others, you will find that most couples are very positive and welcome exploring the deeper aspects of their relationship through the crystals, However, take care that you are not drawn to give an opinion as to the rightness of the course of either person or as referee in a long-standing power battle.

✣ Afterwards cleanse and recharge your crystals, as joint readings absorb a lot of psychic energy.

Geraldine and Linda's reading

Geraldine and Linda live and work in London and have been together for ten years, since their early twenties. Linda wants to have a baby by artificial insemination, using Tom, a friend that they have known for years as a donor. However, Geraldine is reluctant to involve someone so close, as she fears that Tom may develop a special relationship with the baby, as opposed to being one of the many friends of both sexes who will welcome the baby into their circle. Geraldine wants an anonymous donor. But Linda feels that though the baby will be theirs, it is not fair for the baby not to know who his or her biological father is.

Linda selects a **receptive yellow crystal**, a **rutilated quartz**. As Geraldine holds it, she says that she feels as though she is within a crystalline cave, beneath the sea, trapped by yellow tendrils. In contrast, Linda sees a forest of gold that parts to offer a variety of paths, each equally exciting.

Receptive yellow indicates a lack of communication – or, as here, completely different perceptions of the situation that neither women has been able to communicate to the other. Geraldine says that she feels excluded by the fact that the baby will be biologically Tom's, although he will not be directly involved in the upbringing of the baby. Linda feels that the way should be left open for the baby in the future to explore the issues of who are its parents. Tom is quite happy for the baby to know of the connection, although Geraldine will adopt the baby.

Geraldine selects a **receptive red crystal**, a **red-banded agate**. Linda says that she feels heat, like a desert and can sense herself choking in a sandstorm. Geraldine identifies a blacksmith's forge and can hear the hammer on the anvil and experiences a sense of release. Receptive red crystals are symbols of strength in adversity and the need for patience and perseverance.

But they also hold a great deal of repressed anger and resentment that if released and channelled effectively will provide a powerful catalyst for change. Linda says that she is worried about her future, since she feels that Geraldine is reluctant to change their way of life. But Linda feels that if she does not have a baby soon, it will be too late. Geraldine also says that she is being taken down a road about which she is uncertain and fears that the baby will drive them apart.

Linda selects a **creative green crystal,** a **malachite**. Geraldine takes the crystal and visualises a forest with creepers holding her back from seeing the sunlight and the path ahead. In contrast Linda has a sense of delight and sees a picture of clear rivers flowing into a green ocean with water babies swimming round. The stone is one of following your heart which for Linda is having a baby but for Geraldine, she admits for the first time to Linda, is travelling around, developing their photographic agency into the holiday market. So the issue has moved far beyond whether Tom should be the donor to whether the couple really want to have a baby at all.

Geraldine picks a **receptive blue lace agate** a stone that gives them both a sense of joy and freedom. Linda pictures a blue bird soaring high and Geraldine a boat going across mile after mile of pale blue sea. It is a crystal of compromise, of healing and gentleness and shows that here is a reminder that there is a great deal of love between them. It is a question of finding a way forward that enables them both to feel fulfilled. Each, after holding the crystal, says she will go along with the other's plans if that is what is needed to preserve the relationship.

Linda selects a **receptive purple** stone, an **amethyst**. Geraldine visualises a purple sunset over sand and senses herself visibly relaxing and doubts melting away. Linda sees purple grapes in vineyards, olives and orange trees, and both recall the wonderful holiday they spent two years earlier in southern Spain. They have not had a holiday since through pressure of work. The crystal is one of rest and creative withdrawal, and so they decide spontaneously to take a month off, leaving their able assistants in charge, to go back to Spain. This will enable them to discuss the future and to see whether, given the portable nature of babies, the two dreams are compatible.

The final stone which Geraldine chooses is another powerful healing and reconciliatory crystal, a **receptive pink rose quartz**. Linda sees acre upon acre of pink rose bushes and can sense the overpowering fragrance. Geraldine sees the garden of their first home, a cottage in the country and wonders whether there is any way they could move away from London to recapture the earlier, slower and more contented days of their relationship.

Linda acknowledges that she is under increasing pressure from her mother who is eager for a grandchild, and this, Linda says, has created at least part of her sense of urgency to have a child sooner rather than later. In a sense the choice of Tom as donor is, Geraldine points out, an attempt to conform to the world that her mother, who lives in a remote country village in Wales, still tries to impose on Linda. Linda's mother still hopes that her daughter will marry Tom. The issue is much more complex than it seems and the last crystal suggests that Linda needs to shed her unnecessary guilt that her life has not followed the path her mother ordained, so that she and Geraldine can decide what they as a couple really want.

The crystals and astrology

The ancient Egyptians were probably the first to have special 'lucky' stones and a set of 12 different stones was found on a breastplate (excavated from a tomb dating from about 4000 BC) that was worn by the High Priest of Memphis. Thereafter the Hebrews adopted the idea, assigning a stone to each of the 12 tribes of Israel which the High Priest wore in four rows. The tradition evolved to associate a gem or crystal with each of the 12 angels, then to the 12 apostles and finally the 12 months of the year. But birthstones as such did not come into popular usage in Europe until the eighteenth century. I have listed precious gem associations where relevant as you may wish to have a ring or pendant in your own stone as a talisman. But for magical purposes an associated crystal is equally potent.

The list I give combines several of the traditions where there is agreement, and is one I have adapted over the years as my own research into the subject has increased. While your own stone is the most potent for you, especially during your personal Sun sign period, you can use any of the Sun sign crystals when you need its particular strength or quality. Again, these are most powerful during their own zodiacal period.

You can carry or wear the relevant crystal or sleep with it under your pillow. If you need to increase your self-confidence, sprinkle your personal Sun sign crystal with spring water into which you have mixed a few grains of salt, pass frankincense or dragon's blood incense round it clockwise for courage and draw it through the flame of a candle in your zodiacal colour (see below), to harness the four elements. It will then act as a charm of power and protection. You can do the same for any other birth sign crystals you use, if the need is great or urgent.

Astrological dates vary by a day or two according to the system used. If your birth date lies on the cusp, you can use the crystal of the sign that seems most relevant.

♈ Aries, the Ram (21 March–20 April)
For all matters of the self and of identity, for innovation, assertiveness and action.
Crystals: Bloodstone for determination, also diamond.
Candle colour: Red.

♉ Taurus, the Bull (21 April–21 May)
For material matters and security, also for caution if the way ahead seems hazardous.
Crystals: Rose quartz for patience, also emerald.
Candle colour: Pink.

♊ Gemini, the Heavenly Twins (22 May–21 June)
For communication, learning, choices, adaptability and short-distance travel.
Crystals: Citrine for versatility, also sapphire.
Candle colour: Pale grey or yellow.

♋ Cancer, the Crab (22 June–22 July)
For the home and family, especially for protection and for gentle love and friendship.
Crystals: Moonstone for sensitivity, also pearl.
Candle colour: Silver

♌ Leo, the Lion (23 July–23 August)
For nobility and leadership, sensual pleasures and love affairs.
Crystals: Carnelian for courage, also topaz.
Candle colour: Gold.

♍ Virgo, the Maiden (24 August–22 September)
For efficiency, for bringing order to a chaotic situation, for self-improvement and for healing.
Crystals: Jade for harmony, also peridot.
Candle colour: Green.

♎ *Libra, the Scales (23 September–23 October)*
For justice and the law, for balancing options and priorities, relationships, harmony and reconciliation.
Crystals: Lapis lazuli for wisdom, also opal.
Candle colour: Light blue.

♏ *Scorpio, the Scorpion (24 October–22 November)*
For increasing second sight, for passion, sex and secrets, and for claiming what is rightfully yours in any area of life.
Crystals: Banded agate for unconscious awareness, also aquamarine.
Candle colour: Burgundy.

♐ *Sagittarius, the Archer (23 November–21 December)*
For optimism, for clarity of vision and focus, for long-distance travel and house moves and for expanding horizons.
Crystals: Turquoise for open-mindedness, also zircon.
Candle colour: Yellow.

♑ *Capricorn, the Goat (22 December–20 January)*
For ambitions, perseverance, matters concerning officialdom, loyalty and for the acquisition of money.
Crystals: Garnet for fidelity, also ruby.
Candle colour: Indigo or brown.

♒ *Aquarius, the Water Carrier (21 January–18 February)*
For independence, friendship, creativity and for detachment.
Crystals: Amethyst for integrity, also spinel.
Candle colour: Dark blue.

♓ *Pisces, the Fish (19 February–20 March)*
For developing spiritual awareness and intuition, for divination, especially involving water, and the fulfilment of hidden dreams.
Crystals: Crystal quartz for intuition, also beryl.
Candle colour: White.

DAY 25
Crystals for mothers and children

Crystals and children

Children have an intuitive awareness of crystals and if you buy them for your children (first making sure they are old enough not to put them in their mouths), you will find that even a small child will rub an aching brow with a rose quartz or amethyst or hold a citrine up to the sunlight and laugh with joy. They do not worry about power hands or creative or receptive aspects, and perhaps we only introduce such concepts as mental pointers to recapture that instinctive awareness possessed by children. Rose quartz or amethyst will also prevent nightmares and calm an over-active child.

If you have older children you can ask them each to choose a crystal that is special for them. You can also do this for any young relatives or friends' children. Although the next section refers to pregnant women, you can adapt the suggestions to choose a crystal for a friend or relative's child.

Alternatively, select a crystal to represent what Jung called the 'inner child', the essential person hidden within us – the apparently random choice may highlight unexpected facets of yourself.

If none of these aspects interests you, spend time gazing into an amber or rutilated quartz by candlelight and let happy memories of childhood magic flow through you once more.

Crystals and pregnancy

In pregnancy a relationship begins with the unborn child almost from conception – some women even have dreams and visions of their child before conception and these can prove remarkably accurate (see my books *Mother Love*, Robinson, 1998 or *The Mother Link*, Ulysses Press US, 1999, for evidence of this remarkable link). Because pregnancy is such a spiritual time, your crystals can become an important tool to make contact with the infant within you. Adoptive parents can also make this connection with their as yet unknown child even if he or she has already been born.

You may find during pregnancy that one particular crystal becomes precious. If so, use it, for it may be the spiritual crystal of your child, even if it is not their officially designated birthstone. For this reflects the potential child whose actual birthdate can be affected by many factors. Certainly this chosen stone may reflect characteristics you may see as your baby unfolds into a person.

But if you cannot decide on a stone, place your bag of divinatory crystals on your growing womb and, closing your eyes, ask the baby to guide you to his or her special crystal. You may feel a tiny kick or flutter.

Take your time and you will feel one crystal becoming warm and you will know this is the chosen one.

If you select a creative crystal, your infant will be dynamic and outgoing and will often speak before thinking, but will spread love and happiness to all he or she meets.

A receptive crystal indicates a gentler, more thoughtful response to life, a child who will listen and absorb life's bounties and bring peace.

You can also obtain insights from the crystal colour:

White is for a **visionary**, one who sees life as it could be and whose dreams will hold inspired solutions. He or she is the innovator, always aware of hidden possibilities.

Black is for a **nurturer** who, male or female, will protect the weak and vulnerable, will accept human frailty and integrate disparate people or elements of life.

Red is for **courage**, for one who will fear little and will explore where others draw back, fighting for whatever cause is closest to his or her heart.

Orange is for the **joy-bringer** who will bring laughter to the home and make every day a new experience, bringing positive thoughts to those who doubt or despair.

Yellow is for a **communicator**, one who will talk early in life and never stop; these are children who can explain the most complex issue and extricate themselves from difficult situations with charm.

Green is for a **loving heart**, the child who will inspire and give love and friendship, who will be kind and loyal and even as a young child be sensitive to the feelings of others.

Blue is for the **idealist** who is a natural leader, even in playground games, always eager to see new places. He or she will be generous to a fault and never mean-spirited.

Purple is for the **mystic**, the one whom midwives call an 'old soul', wise, attuned to the unspoken thoughts of others, one who seems to talk with angels and fairies as easily as to Earthly friends.

Pink is for the **peacemaker** who brings harmony to home and family and is, from an early age, a natural healer who has an instinctive feel for the right words to soothe and mend quarrels.

Brown is for the **child of the earth**, practical, capable, but always concerned for the environment, good with animals and old people, and able to create a garden of flowers and plants from the most barren patch of land.

You may find that you want to choose two crystals from the bag. We all have many facets to our nature and your child may well be talented in two or more directions.

Place the chosen crystal(s) on your womb each night and visualise your infant bathed in coloured light.

If you feel anxious or agitated, connect with your child by gently circling his or her crystal clockwise over the womb.

If the baby keeps you awake by kicking day and night, as my five did, use crystals in receptive blue, green, pink or purple, especially if your infant's own crystal is a vibrant red or yellow.

You might like to take your baby's crystal to the scan and make a mobile of tiny crystals to hang over the cot with bells to ring in the wind. In earlier times bells were believed to keep all harm from the newborn child.

Crystals and childbirth

Take your baby's crystal with you when you go into labour, as his or her first gift, and circle the bed or add to the birthing pool crystals of your own, red for energy, green for the heart, yellow for the mind, purple to welcome the child's spirit and white for the Life Force.

Afterwards, even in the most regimented impersonal hospital ward, you can hold crystals above your baby as he or she focuses, for it is now known that babies do focus even in those early moments – and who knows what visions an infant beholds? If you get depressed or anxious when the world or hospital routine comes between you and your infant or your private space, you can hold your crystals and know that you are at one with mothers everywhere, retreating into your crystalline pavilion with the baby when the clatter of the ward or visitors becomes too great.

You may like to buy a crystal similar to your baby's special crystal, place it in the ground with a new tree and watch the tree grow as your little one thrives. Or if you live in a flat or apartment, plant the crystal beneath a bonsai tree and each year, on your child's birthday, scatter seeds on waste ground.

The divinatory crystals and their chakras

Women are natural healers, whether soothing a restless or sick child or restoring the bruised ego of a friend or their own urban 'mighty hunter'. Increasingly, medical science is discovering links between the mind, the spirit and the physical body, although there is still the tendency in the westernised world to recommend a physician for bodily ills, a psychiatrist or psychologist for emotional problems and a priest or clairvoyant for dilemmas of the soul. You have already experienced different energies while holding your crystals and it is these varying intensities and emphases that form the basis of *chakra* crystal healing.

What is more, as you have used your crystals for divination and meditation, your crystals have gradually become attuned to your own bodily and spiritual rhythms and so are especially effective for positively influencing your moods and energy flows. One of the most powerful methods of healing you can practise with your divinatory crystals is to give energy to or unblock your chakras.

Chakra is Sanskrit for 'wheel'. The chakras are usually pictured as whirling multi-coloured lotus petals that penetrate both the physical body and the aura, receiving and transmitting energies between body, the Earth and the cosmos. Chakras are part of the Hindu, Tibetan Buddhist and yogic traditions and in the West were first popularised in the late nineteenth century by the Theosophical movement.

The aura is believed to be an electro-magnetic energy field, created by our etheric or inner spirit body. It is generally perceived or felt, with practice, around the outline of the physical body, especially the head, seen around saints and mystics as a golden halo. Auras can extend from a few inches to a vast distance. The aura also acts as a transmitting and receiving station for emotions and thoughts, and reveals information about the physical, mental and spiritual well-being of the individual.

Energy is directed upwards from the all-powerful instinctive and primal *kundalini*. Kundalini is the basic energy that drives the chakras and is pictured as a coiled snake sleeping at the base of the spine until activated consciously by visualisation or spontaneously by intense physical effort. It travels up the body on a spiralling psychic pathway, activating the various energy centres on its journey. Kundalini is identified with the female energy of Shakti, consort of the Hindu god Shiva whom I mentioned in connection with the red crystals.

When the female energy or kundalini reaches the crown chakra, it joins with the male cosmic force, identified with Shiva. Pure white light and spiritual energy is drawn from the cosmos via the crown chakra at the top of the head, so that the mingling and transference of energies creates a state of mental, physical, emotional and spiritual well-being.

This theory is remarkably close to the Jungian *animus* and *anima,* the balance of the assertive and receptive energies in a woman in the correct proportion according to the situation. Sometimes you need a surge of red raw energy when you are fighting, not necessarily for physical survival, but against difficult emotional or verbal odds; it could be a bully at home or work, a threat to your livelihood or your material security, the need to go into work and be dynamic when you have been awake all night with a child or sick relative – or more pleasurably, partying or sharing a night of passion.

At other times you need to be remarkably intuitive and speak from the heart, using pure green heart chakra energy, perhaps to persuade a depressed partner or friend that a betrayal or loss does not mean that he or she has failed or lacks worth, or to push through a project that you passionately believe in.

Each energy centre is linked with particular crystals or colours that can balance deficiencies or clear blockages in the physical and psychic body.

The chakras link with each other and areas of the body they control through *nadis,* thousands of tiny psychic energy lines. The three main symbolic energy channels are called the *sushumna*, the central channel that begins at the base of the spine and rises to an area at the base of the brain, the *ida* and the *pingala* which also extend from the base of the spine to the brow and end at the left and right nostrils. The ida and the pingala criss-cross the sushumna in a spiral like a caduceus, the twined snakes on Mercury's staff.

The universal Life Force is filtered via these channels down the chakras, each of which transforms the energy into the appropriate form for the function it governs. Kundalini rises up the chakra system through the sushumna and contributes primal energy to the higher functions.

When chakras are balanced and healthy, their colours are clear and luminous and they rotate smoothly. However, they can become blocked by external events or inner conflict, becoming cloudy and sluggish, making the area of the body governed by a specific sphere tense or painful, or the whole system prone to infection, and creating a feeling of malaise, depression or anxiety. As a result you may feel 'out of sorts', irritable, and unable to focus on tasks or to find innovative solutions to daily challenges. As these channels operate primarily on a psychic level, there are no definitive paths that are true for all individuals. You may find that at different times you use alternative routes to each chakra, according to the current dominant energy force.

Using the chakra crystals

The seven-chakra system

Traditions vary as to the precise number and names of the chakras. However, the seven-chakra system is one that I find works well in practice and you can use 14 of your divinatory crystals for energising, calming and healing yourself and those you love, by following the chakra method.

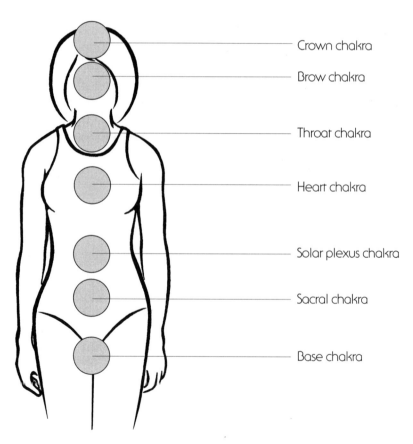

Crown chakra

Brow chakra

Throat chakra

Heart chakra

Solar plexus chakra

Sacral chakra

Base chakra

The root or base chakra, or *maladhara*

This is the Earth or 'instinctive' chakra and its colour is red. It is rooted at the base of the spine, seat of the kundalini or basic energy source. It is linked with your legs, feet and skeleton and the large intestine.

This is the energy centre of the physical level of existence, survival and animal strength. It uses red, raw energy to overcome fearsome odds. Blockages can be reflected in problems with legs, feet and bones, and bowel discomfort. On a psychological level, unreasonable anger at trivial causes can be a symptom.

+ To relieve disorders or to energise any of these organs, use from your divinatory stones an earthy red opaque stone such as red jasper or red tiger's eye or one of the banded red or brown agates, brown tiger's eye or black obsidian or any pebble you find in dark reddish brown to black colouring.

+ Rub your chosen root chakra crystal directly on the skin, from the base of your spine and over your whole skeletal form. Feel the lines of energy and the pull of the Earth of which we are all part. Crystal work can emphasise well-being as well as seek out and dispel ills.

But perhaps your bones ache or you suffer from irritable bowel syndrome or pains in your legs and feet? If it is a pain, there may be a psychic blockage and so you may need some gentle energy to draw out the pain. Panic attacks too may reside here, that may be caused by your instinctive 'fight or flight' mechanisms becoming too easily activated.

+ Concentrate on unblocking or soothing the painful part with a slow, anti-clockwise spiral.

+ If you experience a sudden panic, press your root chakra crystal into the small of your back and leave it there until the panic subsides.

+ Visualise the gentle Earth and deep, volcanic fire warming and soothing your pains away.

The sacral chakra, or *svadisthana*

This is the Moon chakra and its colour is orange. Though seated in the reproductive system, it focuses on different aspects of physical comfort and satisfaction, such as eating, drinking and sexuality. It controls the blood, reproductive system, kidneys, circulation and bladder.

The sacral chakra is the sphere of desire, the chakra of physical pleasure and happiness, and is the home of the five senses. The desire chakra will put you in touch with your ever-reliable 'gut' feelings and help in matters of fertility in the widest sense. Blockages can be reflected in problems with the reproductive system, bladder and circulatory system.

Problems with PMT and menstruation and, for men, impotence, prostate troubles, premature ejaculation and other psychosexual ills can all benefit from contact with sacral crystals. So too can circulation problems, cuts, anaemia and any blood-related conditions. These are excellent crystals to use during pregnancy and childbirth. On a psychological level, irritability and disorders involving physical indulgence can be treated.

✣ For any of these disorders or to energise these organs or boost your circulation, use either an orange glowing crystal, such as carnelian, amber or rich opaque jasper, or banded orange agate or orange sandstone pebbles.

✣ Pass your sacral crystal over your reproductive system, making skin contact, and even if you are no longer physically fertile, feel the Life Force creating new pathways for you to follow.

✣ Trace your veins with a clockwise movement and sense the blood flowing through you, and your fertility and creativity increasing.

✣ If you have a cut or a problem with heavy menstruation, use your orange crystal to slow down the flow. Rotate it anti-clockwise or leave it on the affected chakra area for a few minutes.

When we respond instinctively – and that is not the same as mindlessly – natural physical, creative energies can release power that will extend into relationships and altruistic gestures. Spontaneity is a key to this chakra.

The solar plexus chakra, or *manipura*

This is the Sun or power chakra and its colour is yellow. This chakra is seated just below the navel.

Its body parts include the digestive system, including the liver, spleen, stomach and small intestine. It is said to absorb the Life Force or *prana* from produce such as fruit, vegetables and seeds.

This is the energy centre of digesting experiences, taking what is of use from life and casting aside what is redundant. This chakra comes into its own when you desire power in a situation, or want to achieve an ambition or are planning a career move.

Blockages in this area may be reflected in ulcers, indigestion, problems of the liver, gall bladder, spleen and stomach, yellowy skin and feelings of nausea. Eating disorders such as anorexia and bulimia also have their seat here, when the balance of eating is upset and food necessary for strength and growth becomes attached to an emotional trigger.

On a psychological level, obsessions and over-concern for trivial detail can result.

÷ Run a solar plexus crystal across the skin of your stomach, seat of your gut feelings that are such a good guide in life, and think of the centre of your being absorbing and filtering not only food but impressions from people and from all the senses, including your sixth sense.

Energising yellow crystals can clear the bloated, sluggish feeling sometimes experienced after too many days and nights of artificial lighting, irregular meals, too much coffee, a smoky atmosphere or jarring external noise and tensions. The bright sunlight and sparkling citrines or topaz or yellow zircons are very effective. Agates of any yellow or golden orange shade are especially good for balancing and stabilising energies.

Gentler yellow crystals, such as a moonstone or calcite, can be used to calm this chakra when you are feeling literally churned up by the pressures of life. Stress has a powerful adverse effect on digestion or may cause those tension knots that are manifest as stomach cramps.

See this chakra bathed in gentle golden light, like early morning sunlight after rain.

The heart chakra, or *anahata*

This is the chakra of the winds. Its colour is green and it is situated in the centre of the chest, radiating over heart, lungs, breasts and also hands and arms.

In this chakra, the spiritual nature of the chakras emerges. This chakra controls love, emotions and altruism towards those close to you and to the world generally. The heart chakra can be used for relationship issues and when sympathy and sensitivity are needed.

Blockages can be reflected in heart palpitations, coughs and colds, lung problems and in ailments of the hands and arms. Chesty coughs that go on and on without apparent organic cause, a susceptibility to bronchitis and asthma, as well as irregular heart movements and hyperventilation, can all reside here. On a psychological level, free-floating anxiety or depression can follow an imbalance in this area.

Heart chakra crystals include pink and green stones of all kinds. Green stones range from brilliant green malachite and deep green aventurine to softer jade, amazonite and moss agate.

Pink stones of this chakra include bright rhodonite or rhosochrite, rose quartz and pink kunzite. Pink stones are also associated with the skin and receptive pink stones, especially rose quartz, are excellent for rashes and skin irritations and for warming cold fingers.

 ✢ Pass a heart chakra stone next to your skin around your heart, chest, breast and arms and feel unconditional love, acceptance and harmony flowing freely through your whole being; your lungs are clear and your heart rhythm is steady and strong, flooding your system with green and pink healing light.

✢ If you sense that a physical problem may be rooted in emotion or a physically over-reaction by your system in the form of an allergy, your green or pink crystal can be passed anti-clockwise to draw out misdirected energies and tension.

The throat chakra, or *vishuddha*

This is the chakra of time and space and its colour is blue. It is situated close to the Adam's apple in the centre of the neck. The throat chakra is described as the vehicle for speaking the truth that is in your heart. As well as the throat and speech organs, the throat chakra controls the neck and shoulders and the passages that run up to the ears.

This chakra represents an important transition point from the personal to a wider view of the world. It controls ideas, ideals and clear communication. If things are wrong in this area you may suffer sore throats, colds, swollen glands and thyroid problems. I often get a cold or become hoarse before an important broadcast so I know stress is a vital factor in this area. Blockages can also be reflected in problems with the neck, shoulders, speech organs, mouth, jaw, teeth and throat.

Throat chakra crystals include lapis lazuli, turquoise, aquamarine and blue lace agate, and as the throat is the gateway between the head and body this is a vital chakra for free-flowing energies.

✢ Run a vibrant throat chakra crystal, for example a lapis lazuli or turquoise, across the skin around your throat, jaw, neck and shoulders. Feel the energising blue clearing indecision so that you hear the words you want or need to say emerge from your lips in a confident, wise and non-confrontational way.

✢ Use a softer blue throat chakra crystal, such as blue lace agate or an aquamarine, to relieve sore throats and painful glands or to lessen the effects of a cold. Or you can apply it in an anti-clockwise circle over aching tense shoulders or neck muscles and feel the knots melt.

The brow chakra, or *savikalpa samadhi*

This is the chakra of freedom and its colour is indigo/purple.

The brow or Third Eye chakra is situated just above the bridge of the nose in the centre of the brow, and controls the eyes, ears and both hemispheres of the brain. This is the centre of inspiration and an awareness of a world beyond the material and immediate. The brow chakra controls the psychic functions attributed to the 'Third Eye', i.e. prophetic dreams and harmony. When this chakra is not functioning properly you may experience a lot of headaches, earache, noises in your ears, eye infections or temporary blurring of vision that has no organic cause. On a psychological level, insomnia or nightmares can result.

Brow chakra crystals include amethyst, sodalite, sugilite and peacock's eye (bornite).

+ Sharpen your mind, psychic awareness and intuition and improve your memory by rubbing a vibrant brow crystal, such as a deep amethyst or opaque sugilite, clockwise directly on to your brow into the place of the Third Eye and let sensations come. You may see soft rainbow colours or faint sounds, even music, and you will momentarily connect with past and future. You will also become acutely aware of the wider implications of any present-day decisions.

+ If you cannot sleep, suffer from bad dreams or free-floating anxiety, especially during the night, use a softer brow chakra crystal such as a pale amethyst or purple fluorite to soothe you by gently passing it across your brow.

+ If you have a headache, rub your amethyst dipped in cold water anti-clockwise across your temples, between your eyes or directly on the area of discomfort, to draw out the pain.

The crown chakra, or *nirvakelpa samadhi*

This is the chakra of eternity and its colour is violet/white. White, the source of pure light (all the other colours combined), pours upwards and outwards into the cosmos, and downwards and inwards from the cosmos back into the crown.

The crown chakra is situated at the top of the head in the centre, and rules the brain, body, psyche, growth, and physical, mental and spiritual well-being. It is the centre of creative and spiritual energy and represents either pure spiritual awareness or complete happiness in Earthly terms. Its uses are for making dreams into reality and for finding true personal happiness rather than success on other people's terms.

Blockages can be reflected in problems with sinuses, skin and scalp and general viruses and infections in the whole body that do not clear. You may feel tired but unable to relax, or worried but unable to focus your actions on solutions. You may suffer a series of minor accidents and have a permanent cold. You may feel alienated from friends and family. On a psychological level, an inability to rise above everyday and material concerns and a rigid attitude can result.

The best crystal for connecting with this chakra is clear quartz, a brilliant purple sugilite, also a brow chakra crystal or a rich deep violet and white-banded amethyst.

Wearing a clear crystal quartz around the neck can help to keep this chakra clear. If you also point a crystal quartz towards you while you sleep, or suspend it on a wire above your head in bed, it will enable the pure energies to flow from the cosmos. A cloudy quartz at the foot of the bed, pointing away from you, will enable stale energies to be filtered away. Wash your crown chakra crystals frequently.

Chakra crystals and their associations

The root or base chakra, or *maladhra*	Red
Rooted in the base of the spine, seat of the kundalini or basic energy source. It is linked with your legs, feet and skeleton and the large intestine.	Earthy red opaque stones such as red jasper and red tiger's eye; one of the banded red/brown agates, such as brown tiger's eye and black obsidian.
The sacral chakra, or *svadisthana*	**Orange**
Located in the reproductive system, it focuses on different aspects of physical comfort or satisfaction, such as eating, drinking and sexuality. It controls the blood, the reproductive system, kidneys, circulation and bladder.	Orange glowing crystals such as carnelian, amber or rich opaque jasper,banded orange agate or orange sandstone pebbles.
The solar plexus chakra, or *manipura*	**Yellow**
Seated just below the navel. Its body parts include digestion, the liver, spleen, stomach and small intestine. It is said to absorb the Life Force or prana from living food such as fruit, vegetables and seeds.	For energising: sparkling citrines, topaz or yellow zircons. Agates of any yellow or golden orange shade are especially good for balancing and stabilising energies. To soothe: gentler yellow crystals, moonstones or calcite.
The heart chakra, or *anahata*	**Green**
Situated in the centre of the chest, radiating over heart, lungs, breasts and also hands and arms. Controls emotions.	Pink and green stones of all kinds. Green stones range from brilliant green malachite or deep green aventurine to softer jade, amazonite and moss agate. Pink stones include bright rhodonite or rhosochrite, rose quartz, pink kunzite. Receptive pink stones, especially rose quartz, are excellent for rashes and skin irritations and for warming cold fingers.
The throat chakra, or *vishuddha*	**Blue**
Situated close to the Adam's apple in the centre of the neck. Described as the vehicle for speaking the truth that is in your heart; as well as the throat and speech organs, the throat chakra controls the neck and shoulders and the passages that run up to the ears.	Lapis lazuli, turquoise, for clearing physical and mental blockages; aquamarine and blue lace agate to relive sore throats, painful glands, lessen the effects of a cold. They also help aching, tense shoulders or neck muscles.
The brow chakra, or *savialpa samadhi*	**Indigo/purple**
Located just above the bridge of the nose in the centre of the brow; controls the eyes, ears and the psychic functions attributed to the Third Eye, i.e. prophetic dreams and harmony.	Amethyst, sodalite, sugilite and peacock's eye (bornite), darker and more vibrant shades for psychic awareness and improved memory, paler hues to relieve headaches and anxiety.
The crown chakra, or *nirvakelpa sumadhl*	**Violet/white**
Situated at the top of the head in the centre and rules the brain, body and psyche, growth and well-being, physical, mental and spiritual.	Clear quartz, brilliant purple and sugilite, a rich deep violet and white-banded amethyst or for gentler energies, a cloudy quartz.

DAY 28

Chakra crystals and your well-being

You will have noticed in the list on the preceding pages that receptive and creative crystals were associated with the different chakras functioning.

✢ Take a creative and receptive stone to represent each of the seven chakras, using the list to help you choose. They will not necessarily be the same colour, as for example the root chakra was represented by red, brown and black crystals.

✢ Arrange the crystals in pairs on a bedside table or your window ledge, to correspond with the chakra positions on the diagram on page 140, with the receptive crystal on the left.

✢ Visualise the different coloured crystal energies pouring into their relevant chakras, merging into a rainbow of light, removing blockages, restoring the balance between mind, body and spirit, and giving you power to face the new day. Your dreams may be full of colours and lights.

✢ If you find visualisation difficult, light candles in the main chakra colours and stand them between each pair of crystals for a few minutes before you sleep.

✢ In the morning, wash the crystals after use under running water. Let them dry naturally in sunlight and return them to the bag, placing flowers or greenery next to your divinatory bag to restore the Life Force.

✢ You may decide to buy special crystals to use for chakra work and keep them in a special bag, but in practice your healing chakra work will add new dimensions to your crystal divination, and vice versa.

✢ To promote general well-being, hold the creative chakra crystal over each of its appropriate chakras in turn as you visualise coloured light pouring into the chakra circle.

✢ If you prefer, lie with your creative chakra crystals in place on all seven chakra points and let the rainbow of colours swirl round. This can be very effective if you wake tired after a restless night or must do without sleep for a while.

✢ If you suffer from insomnia, use your receptive chakra crystals to soothe you to sleep and visualise each shutting down an energy centre, beginning with the crown of your head, until there is just the gentle stirring of the kundalini energy at the base of the spine.

Chakra crystal healing

This can heal a specific ailment while you sleep, or help you gain strength for a particular aspect of your life. It may be useful if any chakra is relevant for an encounter the following day, or if an area of your physical well-being needs attention.

✢ Light a candle in the colour of the associated chakra, and place your creative chakra crystals in a circle round the candle with the appropriate creative chakra crystal in the centre.

✢ Pass the chakra crystal you need through the flame and when the crystal is cool, place it a few centimetres from the appropriate chakra.

✢ If you need strength or energy, circle the chakra clockwise nine times with the creative crystal. If there is tension, pain or stiffness to remove, use an anti-clockwise movement.

✢ Blow out the candle, sending the coloured light directly into the crystal.

✢ Replace the chakra crystal in the centre of the circle with some living thing of the same colour – a flower, a plant, a fruit or some seeds – and at bedtime place the crystal beneath your pillow.

✤ In the morning, carry out the same ceremony out of doors using daylight instead of candlelight, making the crystal circle and placing the chakra crystal in the centre next to the living colour.

✤ If it is a sunny day, hold your crystal so that sunlight passes through it, or if not, use what light there is.

✤ Hold the crystal over the appropriate chakra and feel the blockage clearing and energy and optimism pouring in.

✤ Carry the crystal with you. If possible, leave it so that it can absorb natural rather than artificial light.

✤ Hold it over the chakra at noon and again at dusk or until the need has passed.

✤ When several areas of the body are involved in a disorder, or the cause is a mixture of organic and environmental problems, you can use a crown chakra crystal.

Absent healing

You can send love and healing to absent friends and family members using chakra healing. You may already know what is wrong, but sometimes disease, whether of body, mind, spirit or all three, can have its roots in what seems an unrelated area of the body.

✤ Begin by placing your 14 chakra divinatory crystals in the bag and visualising the friend or family member who needs healing. If you have a photograph or personal memento, use that as a focus.

✤ Choose from the bag, by touching each stone but not looking at the crystals, the one that seems to encapsulate the area that needs strengthening.

✤ Place this in the centre of the circle and surround it with your other chakra crystals, beginning with the crown chakra crystals, creative followed by receptive, through to the red; encircle these with candles of the seven main chakra colour correspondences and light the white candle first and the red one last.

✢ Turn towards the place where the person lives, and visualise them in a particular room or area of the garden, projecting a picture of them into the central chakra crystal or placing the photograph next to it. Ask, either silently or using your own words, for whatever healing that is needed to be sent to them from your chakra crystal.

✢ Finally, blow out the candles in the reverse order that you lit them, sending the rainbow beams to the person who is the focus of the ritual and anyone else you know who is in need of healing.

Contact healing

You can also use your chakra divinatory crystals directly for healing those you love, your children, a partner or lover, close relatives or friends. We can all heal those we love, using the powerful telepathic channels of emotion that link us psychically. But if you do want to heal others outside your immediate circle, I would strongly recommend that you contact one of the healing associations that I have listed at the back of the book for professional training.

✢ Ask where the discomfort is felt, although if you are healing your children they may not be able to describe it precisely.

✢ Make the person you are healing comfortable, perhaps lying on their stomach on a bed or couch.

✢ Holding your creative crown chakra crystal in your right hand about 5 centimetes (2 inches) from the body, begin at the point of discomfort and hold your crystal over it.

✢ Turn your crystal anti-clockwise and visualise the pain or discomfort rising as a dark mist or a grey piece of wool, tugging until it is free. Cast it mentally into the cosmos to form a star.

✢ Rotate the crystal clockwise to replace the pain with healing energies, seeing pure white light energies pouring through the crystal into the body.

✢ Allow your crystal to move spontaneously from this spot towards the feet and then to the head. Stop each time you sense a blockage, which may be experienced as an anti-clockwise swirl of energy or heaviness that slows the crystal.

✢ At this point, repeat the cleansing and recharging process.

✢ Ask the person now to lie on their back and repeat the process. Afterwards you may detect a clear, rainbow glow around the whole body, especially around the head, which indicates that the auric field is now much healthier.

✢ If there is a chronic condition, you may need to repeat the process several times. Remember that everyone has a unique system of pathways, so trust your crystals to guide you.

✢ If a blockage is great, use first your crown chakra crystal in your right hand and the receptive chakra crystal that rules the area of discomfort in your left hand. Remove negative energies anti-clockwise, first with the crown chakra and then the ruling chakra crystal, then energise first with the receptive chakra crystal and finally with the crown crystal, clockwise.

Further reading

Crystal healing and divination

Luc Bourgault, *The American Indian Secrets of Crystal Healing*, W. Foulsham & Co., 1997.

Scott Cunningham, *Encyclopaedia of Crystal, Gem and Metal Magic*, Llewellyn, St Paul, MN, 1991.

Soozi Holbeche, *The Power of Gems and Crystals*, Piatkus, 1995.

J. S. Stuart, *The Colour Guide to Crystal Healing*, Quantum, 1997.

Auras and chakras

Ted Andrews, *How to See and Read the Aura*, Llewellyn, 1994.

Barbara Ann Brennan, *Hands of Light, A Guide to Healing through the Human Energy Field*, Bantam, 1987.

Naomi Ozaniec, *The Elements of the Chakras*, Element, 1989.

Candles

Ray Buckland, *Advanced Candle Magick*, Llewellyn, 1997.

Ray Buckland, *Practical Candleburning Rituals*, Llewellyn, 1982.

Cassandra Eason, *Candle Power*, Blandford, 1999.

Herbalism, magical oils and incenses

Nicholas Culpeper, *Culpeper's Colour Herbal*, W. Foulsham & Co., 1983.

Scott Cunningham, *Encyclopaedia of Herbs*, Llewellyn, 1997.

Scott Cunningham, *The Complete Book of Oils, Incense and Brews*, Llewellyn, 1993.

Useful addresses

Crystals

Australia
The Mystic Trader
125 Flinders Lane
Melbourne 3000
Tel: 03 650 4477
Mail order as well as personal
service

South Africa
The Wellstead
1 Wellington Avenue
Wynberg
Cape 7300
Tel: 797 8982
Mail order

Topstone Mining Corporation CC
PO Box 20
Simonstown 7975
Tel: 0121 86-2020/1/2/3

United Kingdom
The Mystic Trader
60 Chalk Farm Road
London
NW1 8AN
Tel: 0171 284 0141
Mail order

Mysteries
7 Monmouth Street
London
WC2H 9DA
Tel: 0171 240 3688
Shop/mail order, everything for
the New Age, plus good advice

USA
Eye of the Cat
3314 East Broadway
Long Beach
CA 90803
Tel: 213 438 3569
Mail order crystals and other New
Age commodities

The Crystal Cave
415 West Foothill Boulevard
Claremont
CA 91711
Mail order. Stocks a huge variety
of crystal and stones, including
unusual ones.

Meditation/visualisation music

Australia
New World Productions
PO Box 244 WBO
Red Hill
Queensland 4059
Tel: 007 33667 0788
Mail order

United Kingdom
Beechwood Music
Littleton House
Littleton Road
Ashford
TW15 1UU
Music of pan pipes, rainforest,
surf and whales

Meditation/visualisation music

USA
Raven Recordings
Room 1815
744 Broad Street
Newark
New Jersey
07102
Tel: 201 642 7942
Meditation music, videos and
tapes

Spiritual healing

Canada
National Federation of Spiritual
Healers (Canada)
Toronto
Ontario
Tel: 284-4798 for information

United Kingdom
British Alliance of Healing
Associations
Mrs Jo Wallace
3 Sandy Lane
Gisleham
Lowestoft
Suffolk
NR33 8EQ
Tel: 01502 742224

National Federation of Spiritual
Healers
Old Manor Farm Studio
Church Street
Sunbury on Thames
Middlesex
TW16 6RG
Tel: 01932 783164

USA
World of Light
PO Box 425
Wappingers Falls
NY 12590
Tel/Fax: 914 297 2867 for a list of
healers

Index